Beginning Ethical Hacking with Python

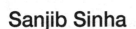

Sanjib Sinha

Apress®

Beginning Ethical Hacking with Python

Sanjib Sinha
Howrah, West Bengal, India

ISBN-13 (pbk): 978-1-4842-2540-0   ISBN-13 (electronic): 978-1-4842-2541-7

DOI 10.1007/978-1-4842-2541-7

Library of Congress Control Number: 2016963222

Managing Director: Welmoed Spahr
Lead Editor: Nikhil Karkal
Technical Reviewer: Abir Ranjan Atarthy
Editorial Board: Steve Anglin, Pramila Balan, Laura Berendson, Aaron Black,
    Louise Corrigan, Jonathan Gennick, Robert Hutchinson, Celestin Suresh John,
    Nikhil Karkal, James Markham, Susan McDermott, Matthew Moodie, Natalie Pao,
    Gwenan Spearing
Coordinating Editor: Prachi Mehta
Copy Editor: Larissa Shmailo
Compositor: SPi Global
Indexer: SPi Global
Artist: SPi Global

Distributed to the book trade worldwide by Springer Science+Business Media New York, 233 Spring Street, 6th Floor, New York, NY 10013. Phone 1-800-SPRINGER, fax (201) 348-4505, e-mail orders-ny@springer-sbm.com, or visit www.springeronline.com. Apress Media, LLC is a California LLC and the sole member (owner) is Springer Science + Business Media Finance Inc (SSBM Finance Inc). SSBM Finance Inc is a **Delaware** corporation.

For information on translations, please e-mail rights@apress.com, or visit www.apress.com.

Apress and friends of ED books may be purchased in bulk for academic, corporate, or promotional use. eBook versions and licenses are also available for most titles. For more information, reference our Special Bulk Sales–eBook Licensing web page at www.apress.com/bulk-sales.

Any source code or other supplementary materials referenced by the author in this text are available to readers at www.apress.com. For detailed information about how to locate your book's source code, go to www.apress.com/source-code/. Readers can also access source code at SpringerLink in the Supplementary Material section for each chapter.

Printed on acid-free paper

DR. AVIJIT SEN, DRISTIPRADIP, KOLKATA.

(For Bringing Light into Darkness)

Contents at a Glance

Contents

About the Author

Sanjib Sinha writes stories and codes—not always in the same order.

He started with C# and .NET framework and won a Microsoft Community Contributor Award in 2011. Later, the Open Source Software movement attracted him and he became a Linux, PHP, and Python enthusiast, specializing in and working on White Hat Ethical Hacking.

As a beginner, he had to struggle a lot—always—to find out an easy way to learn coding. No one told him that coding is like writing: imagining an image and bringing it down to Earth with the help of words and symbols.

All through his books he has tried to help beginners from their perspective—as a beginner.

About the Technical Reviewer

Abir Ranjan Atarthy is a Certified Ethical Hacker from Ec-Council, ISO27001 Auditor and PCIDSS implementer.

He has more than 12 years of extensive domain experience in driving the Information & Cyber Security programs in all key aspects i.e. Policy, Standards, Procedures, Awareness, Network Security, Web security, Android App Security, Incident Response, Security Analytics, Security Monitoring, Malware protection, Security configuration, Cryptography, Data Protection Knowledge of most advanced tools in security industry with complementing knowledge on scripting languages to manually exploit vulnerabilities.

He has authored several technical articles which have been published in IT security journals and is frequently invited to speak at many cyber security conferences and Python forums.

He has designed cyber security courses for Corporates on network and web penetration testing, forensics, and cryptography.

Abir regularly conducts work-shops, training sessions and certification programs for corporates, government organizations, defence establishments, security agencies, engineering colleges and universities on Python programming, penetration testing and cyber forensics.

He has created several IT security and cryptographic tools using Python.

He has accomplished short term Programs in Object-oriented programming and Selected Topics in Software Engineering from Indian Institute of Technology -Kharagpur.

Abir is considered a subject-matter expert in cyber security and is often quoted by leading newspapers and TV channels.

Presently he is leading the Cyber threat intelligence department in TCG Digital Solutions Pvt. Ltd.

Acknowledgments

KARTICK PAUL, SYSTEM MANAGER, AAJKAAL, KOLKATA, Without his persistent and inspiring help, I could not write this book.

Prologue – Hacker's Goal

This book is intended for complete programming beginners or general people who know nothing about any programming language but want to learn ethical hacking.

Let us clear it first: Ethical Hacking is not associated with any kind of illegal electronic activities. They always stay within laws. This book is intended for those people – young and old – who are creative and curious and who want to develop a creative hobby or take up internet security profession acting as ethical hacker. Keeping that in mind we'll also learn Python 3 programming language to enhance our skill as ethical hackers.

This book is not intended for any kind of malicious user. If anyone tries to use this book or any type of code examples from this book for illegal purpose this book will take no moral responsibility for that malicious behaviours.

If you think that you can use this book for any malicious purpose then you are advised to read the first chapter "Legal Side of Ethical Hacking". I hope you won't like the idea of ending up in jail by harming some other systems.

I would like to start this brief introduction with an image. This image depicts many things that I will later discuss in detail. It says, "The author is using "Ubuntu" Linux distribution as his default operating system. He has installed Virtual Box - a kind of virtual machine – that runs in Windows also. And in that Virtual Box he has installed three more operating systems. One is "Windows XP" and the other two are "Kali Linux" and "Windows 7 Ultimate". The image also says, and that is very important, "Currently three operating systems are virtually running on the desktop".

(The virtual Box is running three operating systems. You can try any kind of experiment on this Virtual OS. That will not damage your main system.)

As an ethical hacker you will learn how to defend yourself. To defend yourself sometime you need to attack your enemy. But it is a part of your defense system. It is a part of your defense strategy. More you know about your enemy's strategy, more you can defend yourself. You need to learn those tools are frequently used by the malicious hackers or crackers. They use the same tool that you use to defend yourself.

Whether you are an ethical hacker or a malicious cracker, you do the same thing. You use the identical software tools to attack the security system. Only your purpose or intention differs.

Probably you know that a big car company before launching a new model of car generally tests the locking system. They have their own security engineers and besides they call for the locking experts to test the vulnerability. They pay a good amount of money if you can break the locking system of the car. Basically it is a work of "PENTESTING". The locking experts PENTESTS the system and see if there is any weakness in the system.

It is good example of ethical hacking. The locking experts are invited to do the job and they are paid well. On the contrary car thieves do the same job without any invitation. They simply break the locking system of an unattended car parked on the road side and take it away. I hope by now you have understood the difference between ethical hacking and cracking.

Your main intention centers on the security of the system. Security consists of four key components. As the book progresses you will increasingly be finding words like "PENTESTING", "EXPLOIT", "PENETRATION", "BREAK IN THE SYSTEM", "COMPROMISE THE ROUTER" etcetera. The four key components mentioned below mainly deal with these terms. The key components are:

1. Availability

2. Integrity

3. Authenticity

4. Confidentiality

We will see how crackers want to attack these components to gain access to the system. Since a hacker's main goal is to exploit the vulnerabilities of the system so he wants to see if there is any weakness in these core components.

Let us assume the hacker wants to block the availability of the data. In that case he will use the "Denial of Attack" or 'DoS' method. To do this attack usually hackers use system's resource or bandwidth. But DoS has many other forms. When the resource or bandwidth of your system is eaten up completely, the server usually crashes. The final target is one system but the number of victims is plenty. It is something like millions of people gather in front your house main door and jam it with a kind of human chain so that you and your family members can not enter into it.

The second key component Integrity should not be compromised at any cost. What does this term "integrity" mean? It's basically centered on the nature of data. When this nature of data is tampered with some kind of 'BIT-FLIPPING' attacks, the integrity of the system is also compromised. It can be done just by changing the message itself. The data may either be in the move or at rest, but it can be changed. Imagine what happens when a transaction of money is tampered with the addition of few more zeroes at the end! Let us assume a bank is transferring money. In its instruction it is written: "transfer $10, 000". Now the attacker changes the cryptic text in such a manner so that the amount changes to $10, 000000. So the attack is intended for the message itself or a series of messages.

The issue of authentication is normally handled by the Media Access Control (MAC) filtering. If it is properly placed the network does not allow unauthorized device. What happens if someone spoofs the MAC Address of a legitimate network station and takes it off? He can take on the station's identity and control it. This is called authentication attack or MAC Address spoofing.

Finally the issue of confidentiality rises above all. Data travel in clear text across the trusted network. Here data mean information. The information theft like cracking someone's password is confidentiality attack. The data or information is intended for someone but instead of the recipient the hacker gains the access. Actually the cracker steals it when the data is moving across the trusted network as clear text.

PART I

CHAPTER 1

■ ■ ■

Legal Side of Hacking

As time goes by and we progress, our old environment is also changing very fast. It has not been like before when we keep records by entering data into a big logbook and stack them one by one date-wise. Now we keep data in a computer. We don't go to a market anymore to buy anything. We order it over the Internet and payment is made by using credit or debit card. The nature of crime has also changed accordingly.

Criminals used to snatch your data physically before. They now snatch it over the Internet using computers. Now computers have become a new tool for business as well as for traditional crimes. On the basis of which, a term—"cyberlaw"—comes to the fore. As an ethical hacker, the first and most basic thing you should remember is "don't try to penetrate or tamper any other system without asking permission."

You may ask how I would experiment with my knowledge. The answer is Virtual Box. In your virtual machine you may install as many operating systems as you want and experiment on them (The above image depicts Virtual Box and two operating systems running in it). Try everything on them. Trying any virus on your virtual machine will not affect your main system. At the same time you will keep learning about malware, viruses and every kind of possible attack.

A few examples may give you an idea what type of computer crimes are punishable in our legal system.

If you use any software tool to generate a credit card or debit card number, then it is a highly punishable offense. It will invite a fine of fifty thousand dollars and fifteen years of imprisonment. Setting up a bogus web site to take credit card numbers with a false promise of selling non-existent products is a highly punishable offense. Rigorous imprisonment and a hefty fine follow. I can give you several other examples that may invite trouble for you if you don't stay within the law.

Remember, you are an ethical hacker and you are learning hacking tools for protecting your or your client's system. For the sake of protection and defense, you need to know the attack, exploit or penetration methods.

Try every single experiment on your virtual machine.

That is the rule number one of ethical hacking.

Electronic supplementary material The online version of this chapter (doi:10.1007/978-1-4842-2541-7_1) contains supplementary material, which is available to authorized users.

CHAPTER 2

■ ■ ■

Hacking Environment

The very first thing that you need is a virtual machine. As I said before, I have Ubuntu as my default operating system and inside my virtual machine I have installed two operating systems—one is Windows XP and the other is Kali Linux.

Technically, from now on I would mention Windows XP and Kali Linux as my virtual machines. Kali Linux is a Linux distribution that comes up with many useful hacking tools. So I strongly suggest using it as your virtual machine. You may also read the documentation page of Kali Linux, which will also be an immense help.

At the same time, I'd not suggest using Windows of any kind for the ethical hacking purpose. Some may argue that few hacking tools can be used in Windows, so why you are suggesting otherwise? The point is: in the ethical hacking world, you need to be anonymous all the time. You won't want to keep your trail, anyway, so that you can be traced back. Remaining anonymous is a big challenge. In Linux it is fairly easy and you can stay anonymous for the time being.

Keeping that in mind, I explain that technique of being anonymous in great detail so that before jumping up into the big task, you make your defense much stronger. Being anonymous is the most important thing in the world of ethical hacking. Keeping yourself anonymous in Windows is not possible. So it is better to adapt to the Linux environment first. Another important thing is, most of the great hacking tools are not available in the Windows environment.

If you have never heard of any Linux distribution, don't worry. You can either install user-friendly Ubuntu inside your Windows system or you can easily partition your disk into two parts and install Ubuntu and Windows separately as your two default operating systems. It is preferable to do the latter. Installing and uninstalling parallel operating systems always teaches you something new. If you are familiar with Windows, I won't tell you to simply dump it for the sake of learning ethical hacking. You can keep it and use it for your daily work. There is no problem in doing this.

In the Internet world, Linux is used more. So you need to learn a few Linux commands. Software installation in Linux is slightly different from Windows environments. There are Linux distributions like Fedora or Debian, and many more. I named Ubuntu just because it is extremely popular and Windows users find themselves comfortable inside it. The operations are more or less the same, including the software installations. For beginners, it is not a good idea to install Kali Linux as your default OS. You must read Kali documentation, where it is clearly stated that Kali is more for developers. You are going to install it inside your Virtual Box. Kali Linux is a kind of Linux distribution that comes with lot of hacking tools. You need to know them and use them in the course of ethical hacking.

© Sanjib Sinha 2017
S. Sinha, *Beginning Ethical Hacking with Python*, DOI 10.1007/978-1-4842-2541-7_2

Installing Virtual Machine is a very important step as the first step of building your environment. In the next chapter I will show you how you can do that for different operating systems. Another important thing is learning a programming language that will really help you learn ethical hacking better.

The obvious choice is Python. At the time of writing this book, Python 3.x has already arrived and is considered the future of this language. It is very quickly catching up with the old Python 2.x version, which has been around the market for a while. The official Python download page provides the repository of Python installers for Windows, Mac OS X and Linux operating systems. If you download an installer, it is of immense help because it comes with the Python interpreter, standard library, and standard modules. The standard library and built-in modules are specifically very important because they offer you several useful capabilities that will help you achieve your goal as an ethical hacker. Among the useful modules, you will get cryptographic services, Internet data handling, interaction with IP protocols, interoperability with the operating system, and many more. So go ahead, pick up any good beginner's book on Python, read the official documentation and know that it is a part of your learning schedule. Python is an extremely easy language to learn.

To create an ideal ethical hacker's environment, a few steps are extremely important. The steps include: installing Virtual Machine or Virtual Box (VB), having a basic knowledge about networking, and learning a useful programming language like Python. Let us first have a look at the basic networking knowledge.

Ethical Hacking and Networking

A basic knowledge about internetworking is extremely important if you want to learn ethical hacking. As you progress and want to go deeper, it is advisable to learn more about networking. Ethical hacking and internetworking are very closely associated. As you progress through this book you will find words like "packet," "switch," "router," "modem," "TCP/IP," "OSI," and many more.

The very first thing you need to know is: data travels through many layers. Ethical hackers try to understand these layers. Once they have understood the movement, they either want to track and block the data or they want to retrieve data.

In this chapter, we will very briefly see how internetworking models work. We will look into the different types of networking models. We will also learn about the devices that comprise a network.

What Does Network Mean?

A network is a collection of devices that are connected through media. One of the main characteristics of a network is: devices contain services and resources. Devices contain personal computers, switches, routers, and servers, among others. What do they do basically? They send data and get data either by switching or by routing. Actually, they connect users so that users ultimately get full data instead of getting it by pieces. So the basic services these devices provide include switching, routing, addressing, and data access.

We can conclude that a network primarily connects users to avail these services. That is its first job. The second job is also very important. A network always maintains a system so that the devices allow the users to share the resources more efficiently.

Now a problem arises—not a trivial problem. Hardware and software manufacturers don't know each other. They belong to different countries and share diverse cultures. When the conception of networking first came to the fore, it was found that hardware and software weren't matching. As I said before, a network is a collection of devices. These devices are mainly built of hardware and software that are talking in different languages.

To solve this problem, a common network model with communication functions is needed so that dissimilar devices can interoperate.

The importance of internetworking models consists of a few main concepts. First, they encourage interoperability. Second, they provide a reference through which data will be communicated. Third, they facilitate modular engineering.

There are two types of internetworking models.

They are Open Systems Interconnection (OSI) reference model and Transmission Control Protocol/Internet Protocol (TCP/IP) model. Both models are widely used today.

The Open Systems Interconnection (OSI) reference model was developed by the Internet Standards Organization (ISO) and it has seven layers in all. The layers are as follows: application (layer 7), presentation (layer 6), session (layer 5), transport (layer 4), network (layer 3), data link (layer 2) and physical (layer 1).

Let us very briefly try to understand how this model works. Suppose a user tries to open a web page. The very first thing he does is send a request to the server that is located several thousand miles away. Here, the server's hard disk or hardware is the last layer (layer 1) which is termed as "physical." So, the user's request first knocks the "application" layer (7) which is the nearest and then it proceeds. Every process in each layer involves a complicated "bits and bytes" functioning. A computer only understands 0 and 1. But the user does not like to see a video in 0 and 1.

Let us break the process into more detail.

In the application layer (7), the user interacts with the device that could be a personal computer or smart phone or anything you might guess. So the application layer basically handles the user's interaction. The name of the datagram is "data." The user requests the data and ultimately retrieves the data. What happens when the user sends requests from layer 7? It enters into the next layer: (6) presentation. The process of encapsulation starts. Data is formatted and encrypted. Next, the layer 5 or session enters into the scene. This layer manages end-to-end communication. Suppose you type a password and log into your social media account. This layer maintains the end-to-end (user-to-server) communication so that you can remain logged into your page. Tell this layer the name of the datagram is "data."

To assist you in maintaining your session, the next three layers work very hard. They are: transport (layer 4), network (layer 3), data link (layer 2), respectively. The name of the datagram of transport layer is "segment." Why is this called "segment"? It is called "segment" because it breaks your request into several fractions. First, it adds source and destination port numbers. Next, it tries to make it reliable, adding sequence numbers. So, in a nutshell, it provides flow control, sequencing, and reliability.

What happens next?

Your request enters into the layer 3 that is called network. The name of the datagram is "packet." It adds source and destination IP addresses. It also makes sure that your request finds the best path to reach the destination.

7

Now your data request almost reaches the final stage. It enters into the layer 2 that is data link. It is nearing the end point that is the server's hardware. So this layer adds source and destination Media Access Control (MAC) addresses. Next, it goes through Frame Check System (FCS) processes. It checks frame by frame whether the source requests reach the right destination. That is why the datagram is known as "frame."

Now it has entered into the final destination that is layer 1 or physical. There are only bits over the physical medium. The name of the datagram is "bits and bytes."

Now we can imagine a small office with one router, two switches and a few desktops, laptops, printers, and servers. The router is connected to the switches and the switches are connected to the devices like desktops, laptops, printers, and servers. Here desktops, laptops, printers, and servers belong to the layer 1 that is physical. The switches belong to the layer 2 that is data link, and the router fits in the layer 3 that is network.

Routers are layer 3 devices and perform a few definite tasks. They are: packet switching, packet filtering, path selecting, and finally communicating. The task of packet switching involves the process of getting a packet to the next device. Here, the next device is the switches. Packet filtering suggests in its name what it actually does. It either permits or blocks packets depending on certain criteria. Path selecting is determining the best path through the network to the destination. Communication is another important part of this layer. Routers communicate with other networks like the Internet.

Between routers, layer 3 devices, and the end application, physical, layer 1 devices, there are switches which are layer 2 devices. In some cases, switches perform the task of layer 3 devices. Switches basically deal with frame filtering and forwarding. It also maintains the connection between layer 3 and layer 1.

Summary

Let us quickly recap what we have just learned about the relations between ethical hacking and internetworking.

1. Internetworking models encourage interoperability between different devices, providing a reference to describe the data communication. At the same time, it facilitates modular engineering.

2. There are two types of internetworking models. They are OSI Reference Model and TCP/IP Model.

3. The OSI Model has seven layers. They are: application (layer 7), presentation (layer 6), session (layer 5), transport (layer 4), network (layer 3), data link (layer 2), and physical (layer 1).

4. The TCP/IP Model has four layers. They are: application (layer 4), transport (layer 3), network (layer 2), and network (layer 1).

5. An ethical hacker tries to understand this process of data communication and penetrates according to the vulnerability.

CHAPTER 3

■ ■ ■

Installing Virtual Box

The first question that comes to our mind is: why do we need a virtual box when we have a default operating system in place? There are several reasons. The most important reason is: in a virtual box we can play with any operating system without any fear of messing it up, even breaking it up. There is every possibility that while testing a hacking tool we could break a system. I encourage you to do that. It is a virtual machine. So, go ahead. Test everything that comes to your mind. Another great reason for using virtual box is the safety. When you visit a web site. you might consider it to be safe but in reality it could not be so. But nothing matters in the case of a virtual box. It is not your original machine with confidential data. Visiting an unsafe web site is not annoying anymore.

Only one thing you need to remember. Stay within the law. While testing your hacking tools or running codes, you cannot jeopardize any other system.

The Oracle Virtual Box official web site offers plenty of download options. You can choose any one of them. According to your OS, you go to the "download" section and see what is available for you. From the next image you will have an idea how you can proceed further.

Figure 3-1. *Virtual Box download section for Linux hosts*

The selected line of the above image shows the default operating system I am running currently. That is Ubuntu 14.04 (Trusty) and the architecture is AMD64.

Virtual Box is very easy to install. Whatever your OS is (Mac OS X, Windows, or Linux), you can install it. First, you need to know about your operating system itself. It could be either 32-bit or 64-bit architecture. In any Linux distribution, it is extremely easy to learn. Just open up the terminal and type: "uname -a".

The terminal will spit out some vital information that includes all data regarding my current default system. The Linux is of 3.19.0 version and the super user's name is "hagudu." It also indicates what type of system architecture this is. It looks like this:

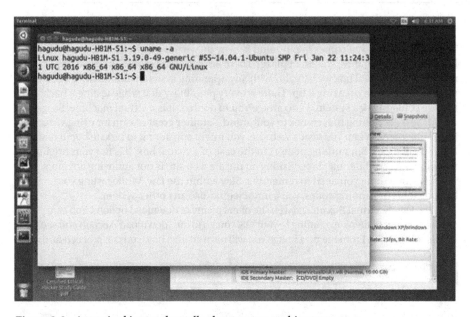

Figure 3-2. *A terminal image that tells about system architecture*

As in my case, you clearly see that "x86_64" stands for 64 bit. In the Virtual Box official download page for all Linux distribution, you first download the required packages and then install it according to the nature of your OS. For Red Hat, Fedora or any Linux distribution belonging to that category, you will notice that the last extension is ".rpm". In that case, you can move to the Virtual Box folder and issue commands like "rpm -i" or "yum install" in case you run Red Hat or Fedora.

But there are more simple methods to install Virtual Box.

For the absolute beginners it is much helpful to run Ubuntu Linux distribution as your default OS. You can install Virtual Box from the software center directly without opening up the terminal or issuing any command.

The Ubuntu software center has many categories. One of them shows the "installed" software.

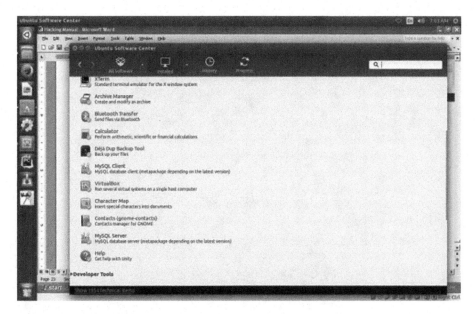

Figure 3-3. *Ubuntu software center shows Virtual Box running*

It is not there by default. In that case, it is extremely easy to install. You can just type "Virtual Box" on the search text box and it will pop up. Move ahead and press the installation button.

CHAPTER 4

■ ■ ■

Installing Kali Linux and Other Operating Systems on VB

Once the Virtual Box has been installed on your machine, you need not worry about installing several operating systems on it. At the very beginning, we are interested about installing Kali Linux on our Virtual Box. Go to the official Kali Linux web site and download the ISO image of the latest stable version. Kali Linux is a much bigger Linux distribution than other Linux distributions. It must be around 3 GB. Ubuntu and others are around 1 GB or a little bit more.

Now once the installation process is over, you can either store it on your local hard drive or burn it on a DVD. Now open up your Virtual Box and click "New". It will automatically open up a new window that will ask you what type of operating system you are going to install. The following image is quite self-explanatory.

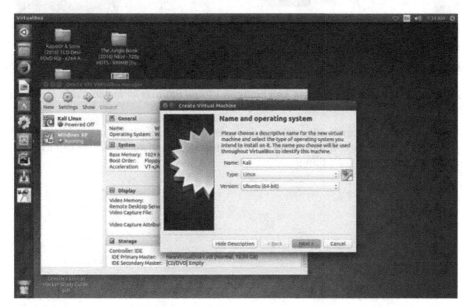

Figure 4-1. How to install an operating system on Virtual Machine

© Sanjib Sinha 2017

S. Sinha, *Beginning Ethical Hacking with Python*, DOI 10.1007/978-1-4842-2541-7_4

You see on the Virtual Box I have already installed two operating systems. One is Kali Linux and the other is Windows XP. In your case, when you are going to install fresh, the left panel of your virtual box will be empty.

The whole procedure is very explicit in itself. It will guide you to do what to do next. Basically, on the Internet there are lots of illustrative guides that will help you do the same thing. Now it is time to write down the name of the operating system you are about to install. Next select the type (whether it is Linux or Windows, etc.) and the version. In the long list of versions section you won't find the name of Kali. But basically it is "Debian." So go ahead and select the 32-bit or 64-bit Debian according to your system architecture. Click "next" and it will ask for the memory usage as it is shown in the next image.

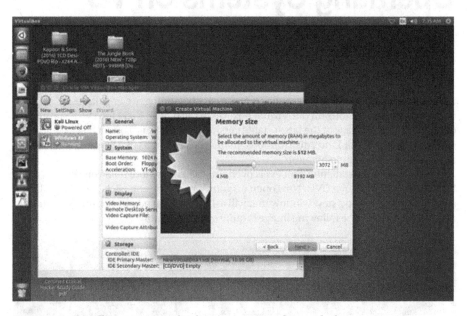

Figure 4-2. Installation process of Kali Linux on Virtual Box asks for memory size

You can allocate the memory size as per your machine capacity. Minimum 1 GB is good. It is better if you can allocate more. In the next step it will ask for storage capacity and a few other nitty-gritty things.

I can assure you, as a complete beginner you won't face any difficulty in installing Kali Linux on your Virtual Box. The most important part of this installation process is you need to keep your Internet connection running so that Kali Linux will adjust its prerequisites accordingly online.

Usually when an operating system is installed on a virtual machine it comes up in a small size and it stays like that. The next image will show you the original size.

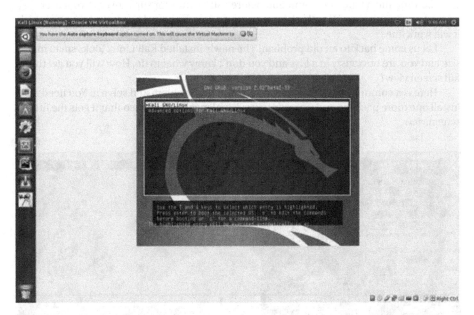

Figure 4-3. *Kali Linux running on Oracle VM Virtual Box*

But working on this size is really cumbersome. To solve this problem, normally Virtual Box Guest Addition is used. But before that, you may want to update and upgrade your newly installed Kali Linux. That is a good practice that helps you to be updated all the time. After you have logged in typing username and password, you will find the terminal on the left panel. Open it and type:

```
apt-get update
```

You must be online so that it will be updated on its own. It might take some time. After it finishes off you issue the second command:

```
apt-get upgrade
```

Normally the upgrading takes more time than updating. If you are a root user then there should not be any problem. But if you have created another user and log in as that user then you must type "su" command before. "su" stands for super user or root user who is the administrator. It will ask for your super user password instantly. You give it and it will work fine.

Let us come back to an old problem. The newly installed Kali Linux looks small in size and you are obviously at a loss and you don't know what to do. How will you get the full screen view?

Here is a command that will rescue you from this problem and solve it. You need to install one more package and upgrade your virtual machine again so that it gets the full screen view.

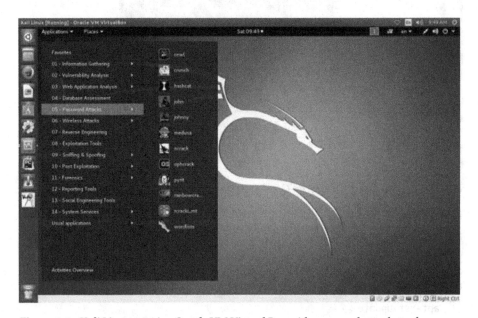

Figure 4-4. *Kali Linux running Oracle VM Virtual Box with password attacks tool*

Open up the terminal and type:

```
apt-get update && apt-get install -y dkms linux-headers - $(uname -r)
```

This will install the necessary package that will run the Virtual Box Guest Addition. It is something that you can imagine as a tool that controls the screen size of your host OS.

How will you run it once the package is installed? The next image will guide you to find the place where you will get it.

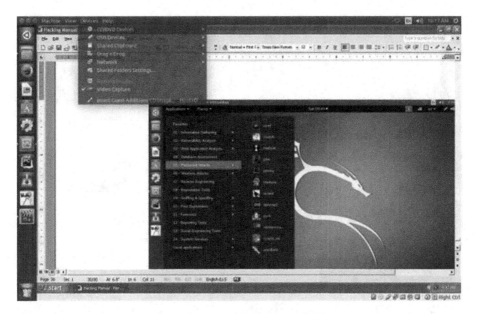

Figure 4-5. *Getting the full screen size of Kali Linux on Virtual Box*

Take your mouse pointer to the upper middle part where you will get the "Devices" menu. The last one reads like this: "insert guest edition CD image." Click it and it will automatically take care of everything.

Normally it should work fine. If not, take it as a challenge. Search the Internet. There are lots of helping hands waiting for you to assist what you want to get.

Now we are going to install Windows 7 Ultimate. The starting process is same. You open the virtual box. Go to "new" and click. It will open up a window that will ask you to type the name of the operating system you are going to install. Next it will ask for the memory size. For Windows 7 Ultimate you need to allocate at least 2 GB. Bigger is better. For the hard disk storage capacity, 50 GB is enough.

Now you are ready to connect to the ISO image of the OS.

This part is a little tricky, but any online guide will show you how you can connect them.

When you click the "storage" section of your Virtual Box it will pop open a window that tells you to connect with the ISO image. It is not at all difficult. The advantage of Virtual Box is if you fail to do some job it won't affect your original machine.

Figure 4-6. *Installation of Windows 7 Ultimate takes place*

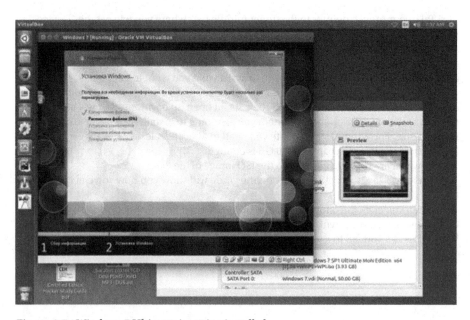

Figure 4-7. *Windows 7 Ultimate is getting installed*

When any new OS is installed on your virtual machine, it is usually small in size. But there is a technique that will help you get the original full screen effect.

For Windows 7 Ultimate, there is a Virtual Box Guest Addition folder available in the storage section. The blue-colored box comes with a label. It reads Virtual Box Guest Additions. Just click on it. It will open up. It will contain several files. You will notice two ".exe" files. One is for the 32-bit and the other is for the 64-bit system architecture. My machine is 64 bit so I click and run it. The steps are very simple. It will ask for it to be installed. Click OK and proceed. It will make your Windows 7 Ultimate virtual machine state full screen.

We have successfully installed Virtual Box on our virtual machine and we have installed Kali Linux and Windows 7 Ultimate on it. Now it's time to move on.

CHAPTER 5

■ ■ ■

Linux Terminal, Basic Commands

It is extremely important to know about the Linux terminal and commands. Not in great detail, but this primary knowledge will help you immensely in the future. The more you delve deep into the world of ethical hacking, the more you will start feeling that you need to know more about the Linux system. This book will not take you that far. But a very basic knowledge is necessary so that you can understand what is going on around you.

It might seem repetitive, but I would like it to be cemented in your mind that without knowing Linux properly you can't go deep into the mysterious world of ethical hacking. So you must know basic commands first. These commands will tell you about the computer itself. It will tell you the location of file system—where you are on your computer. By these commands you can change the permission of a file system, copy, or permanently remove a file. You can add a new user to your system. You can have a listing of files that are currently in the directory where you are. This listing includes the hidden files. In a nutshell, you can at least do the basic operations through your keyboard without using your mouse pointer. That is great from the perspective of a beginner, I presume.

To begin with, let us first start Kali Linux. In the following image you will see a full screen representation of Kali. I am going to explain a few things first, so that as a beginner you will learn what you need to know first about Kali.

© Sanjib Sinha 2017

S. Sinha, *Beginning Ethical Hacking with Python*, DOI 10.1007/978-1-4842-2541-7_5

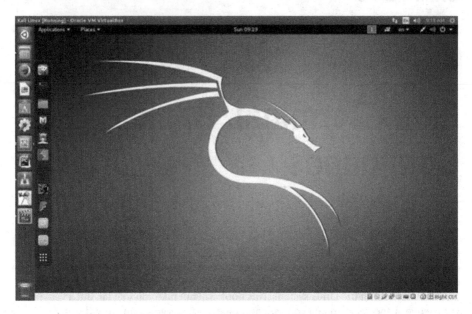

Figure 5-1. *Kali Linux full screen view with its left panel*

The image above is showing the full screen view of Kali Linux. On the left panel on the top, there is the browser, "Iceweasel." Next follows the command line tool. We need that tool pretty often in the coming lessons. The command line tool or terminal basically deals with all types of keyboard inputs. The good programmers hardly use a mouse pointer. They are more comfortable with this terminal and keying. The file system follows it. If you click on it, it will open up a window just like any Windows NT version. You will see various directories and folders like "Home," "Downloads," "Pictures," etcetera.

Let us start with the command tool by opening it. You can make it look bigger. Just use your "control" and "shift" keys with the "+" sign.

In the following image you will see a few starting commands that we usually type to know what kind of files we have in some directories or folders.

What does the image show?

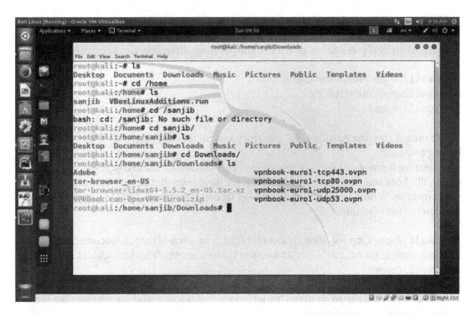

Figure 5-2. *Kali Linux with the command line tool*

It shows that I have typed "ls" first. What does that "ls" command mean? It stands for listing. I tell Kali to show the listing of files and folders that you have and, in a fraction of second, it shows me all it has.

Next I have used the "cd" command. What does that mean?

This "cd" command stands for "change directory." You see in the image that I have changed the directory to "home" and issue the "ls" command again to see what it has. It has one folder called "sanjib" and a file. The folder "sanjib" means the "root" or system itself has a user called "sanjib". Now as a root or administrator, I have created that user so that at the beginning I can log in as "sanjib". You can create several users in a Linux system so that from various machines they can log into their files and folders. But the users will never have the root privilege. They can't penetrate into the administrator's space but the root or administrator can always see what the users are doing. As a root, an administrator can create or delete any user.

From this place you can guess what is happening. We change the directory and look at what "sanjib" has in its directory "Downloads."

Next we learn about the "pwd" command. It states your position. As a root, if you are at "Home" directory and issue a "pwd" command, it has output like this:

```
root@kali:/home# pwd
/home
root@kali:/home#
```

It says you are at "/home" directory. This "pwd" command is important when you have to control a large complicated system. Often you might forget where you are working. Usually if you want to go back to the previous directory, you need to type this:

```
root@kali:/# cd /home/sanjib/
root@kali:/home/sanjib# cd ..
root@kali:/home#
```

It means you first go to "sanjib" directory and then come back with a "cd" command having two dots.

Next we learn about the "cp" command. This command stands for copy. You can copy a file from one destination to the other. We have seen that in our "home" directory we have a file, "VBoxLinuxAdditions.run." Let us copy this file to the "Documents" directory of user "sanjib".

```
root@kali:/home# cp -v VBoxLinuxAdditions.run /home/sanjib/Documents/
'VBoxLinuxAdditions.run' -> '/home/sanjib/Documents/VBoxLinuxAdditions.run'
root@kali:/home#
```

Now we would like to go to the "sanjib" documents folder and see whether the file has been properly copied or not.

```
root@kali:/home# cd sanjib/Documents/
root@kali:/home/sanjib/Documents# ls
VBoxLinuxAdditions.run
root@kali:/home/sanjib/Documents#
```

I have changed the directory to "sanjib/Documents" and issue the "ls" command to see the listing. It shows the file. So it is working properly.

You can learn about any command very easily. You just need to add a "—help" command like this: "cp -help." It spits out everything about that command and it is very verbose. It tells you about any command in full detail.

Another very important command is "mv". With this command, you can move any file from one folder to another folder. This command is more or less like a "cp" command. But there is a major difference. This command completely moves the file from one place to the other. Another important command is "cat." You can read any text file with the help of this command.

I have a folder called "Writing" and have some documents over there. Now with the help of this command we can read any text file. Remember it is true only for a text file. For an experiment, I wanted to read a file with extension ".odt" and the next image shows you how it looked on the terminal.

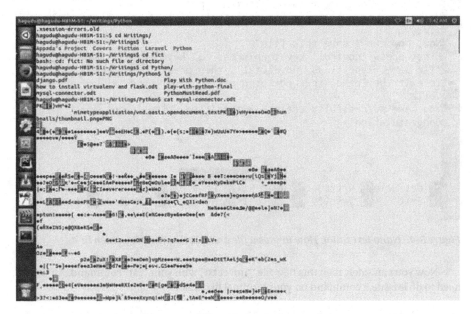

Figure 5-3. *Trying to read a non-text file with "cat" command*

In this part I want to show another trick that is often being used in Linux. Suppose you want to write a text file very quickly. You can use "nano". It comes with every Linux distribution. Just type "nano" on your terminal and it will open up a text editor on the terminal itself. The next image shows you how it happens.

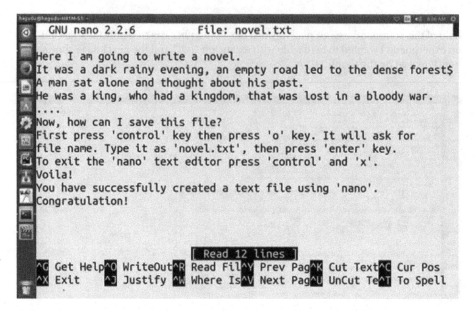

Figure 5-4. *Nano text editor. How to save a file and exit the editor is written in it.*

Now you can safely read this new file, "novel.txt", with your "cat" command. All you need to do is issue a command on your terminal like this:

```
cat novel.txt
```

It will read your file on the terminal itself.

Now it might be a good idea to edit this file. You can edit it on the terminal using "nano". In that case, you need to write on your terminal this command:

```
nano novel.txt
```

This will tell "nano" to open the file. The rest is the same. You can edit any portion and, with the "control" and "o" key, you can save it again. Then you can exit the file with "control" and "x".

In the next image we will see how it looks when we try to read a file by using the "cat" command.

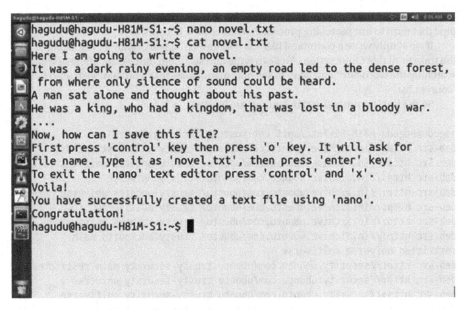

Figure 5-5. *Reading a text file using "cat" command*

Usually, seasoned programmers used to work on the terminal and text editors like "VI," "VIM," or "NANO" are extremely popular.

Now we are going to learn a very important Linux command called "grep". This command does some sort of searching inside a file and it does it in a very interesting manner. Let us first see what we have in our root directory.

We issue a command like this on our terminal and see the output.

```
hagudu@hagudu-H81M-S1:~$ cd /etc/apt
hagudu@hagudu-H81M-S1:/etc/apt$ ls
apt.conf.d      sources.list    sources.list.save  trusted.gpg    trusted.
gpg.d
preferences.d  sources.list.d  trustdb.gpg            trusted.gpg~
hagudu@hagudu-H81M-S1:/etc/apt$
```

As you can see, we have changed the directory to "/etc/apt" and see the listing. We find many files there and presently we are interested in the "sources.list" file. We can use the "cat" command to read the file but we have something different in mind.

We would like to search some particular word and want to separate them and see them in segregation. The command "grep" along with another command, "|" (pipe), will help us in doing so.

We actually tell the terminal to display the content of "sources.list" first and then pipe that term to our searching process. Let us see how it works.

If we simply write a command like "cat sources.list", it will display a long listing of the sources of this Linux system. You can write and see them. But we are interested about searching the word "src" and want to see how many times that word has been used in the "sources.list".

So the final command and the output are like this:

```
hagudu@hagudu-H81M-S1:/etc/apt$ cat sources.list | grep src
deb-src http://in.archive.ubuntu.com/ubuntu/ trusty main restricted
deb-src http://in.archive.ubuntu.com/ubuntu/ trusty-updates main restricted
deb-src http://in.archive.ubuntu.com/ubuntu/ trusty universe
deb-src http://in.archive.ubuntu.com/ubuntu/ trusty-updates universe
deb-src http://in.archive.ubuntu.com/ubuntu/ trusty multiverse
deb-src http://in.archive.ubuntu.com/ubuntu/ trusty-updates multiverse
deb-src http://in.archive.ubuntu.com/ubuntu/ trusty-backports main
restricted universe multiverse
deb-src http://security.ubuntu.com/ubuntu trusty-security main restricted
deb-src http://security.ubuntu.com/ubuntu trusty-security universe
deb-src http://security.ubuntu.com/ubuntu trusty-security multiverse
# deb-src http://archive.canonical.com/ubuntu trusty partner
deb-src http://extras.ubuntu.com/ubuntu trusty main
# deb-src http://archive.ubuntu.com/ubuntu trusty universe
hagudu@hagudu-H81M-S1:/etc/apt$
```

It is interesting to note that we first issued a command like this: cat sources.list | grep src

And the long output that follows that command has all the statements that have "src" in it.

We can even filter the source file more distinctly. We can narrow down our searches more and tell the terminal to find the word "src" only with small letters by writing down this command:

```
cat sources.list | grep -i src
```

In the future, we will use this "grep" command extensively to scan a network with a particular word.

Another important command is "echo". This command literally echoes everything you write on your terminal. You can also do something more with this command. You can even change a text file with this command.

Previously we have written a text file "novel.txt" and saved it on our home directory. Now we are going to overwrite that file with this "echo" command.

```
hagudu@hagudu-H81M-S1:~$ echo "I DON'T LIKE THIS NOVEL ANYMORE SO I CHANGE
IT" > novel.txt
hagudu@hagudu-H81M-S1:~$ cat novel.txt
```

I DON'T LIKE THIS NOVEL ANYMORE SO I CHANGE IT

```
hagudu@hagudu-H81M-S1:~$
```

We have first echoed some text on our terminal, then we used ">" (greater than sign) to put that text into the file "novel.txt". In the next command, we have again used the "cat" command to read the file "novel.txt" and found that the file has been changed.

Now we will learn how to make directories in Linux. There is a very useful command: "mkdir". It plainly means "make directory." Let us make a directory named after this project: "Ethical Hacking." You may guess that the command is extremely simple: mkdir Ethical Hacking

No, it is not. In this case, if you write that way, Linux terminal understands something else. It comprehends that you want to create two separate directories. One is "Ethical" and the other is "Hacking." It has already created two directories in that way. So let us remove them first and next we will create a directory with more meaningful meaning.

To remove a directory, you must have "root" privilege. It means you are an administrator or super user of the system. In Ubuntu, if we want to be a "root" or "super user," we issue the command "sudo" first. In Kali Linux it is different: "su". But in both cases once you write that command, the system will ask for the password through the terminal. Let us see how it works.

We first issue the command and in the next step we check with the "ls" command to see whether those directories exist anymore.

```
hagudu@hagudu-H81M-S1:~$ sudo rm -rf Ethical/ Hacking/
[sudo] password for hagudu:
hagudu@hagudu-H81M-S1:~$ ls
```

It worked—two directories have been removed successfully. Let us try to understand it more. We already know that the "rm" command stands for the word "remove." But what about the "-rf" command that follows it? The command "-rf" means "do it recursively with force." Generally this "-rf" command is used to remove directories. You have to be very careful about using this command because in Linux, once you have used this command, the file or directory is deleted permanently. It is next to impossible to retrieve them. It is wise to be very careful about using it.

Hopefully you have also noticed that we have started our command line with "sudo". And you write "sudo", it asks for the password. In this case, you always give the password that you usually type down to log into the system.

Let us again make the directory properly and this time we name it "Ethical-Hacking", so that the system will no longer interpret it as two separate directories.

```
hagudu@hagudu-H81M-S1:~$ mkdir Ethical-Hacking
hagudu@hagudu-H81M-S1:~$ cd Ethical-Hacking/
hagudu@hagudu-H81M-S1:~/Ethical-Hacking$ ls
hagudu@hagudu-H81M-S1:~/Ethical-Hacking$ touch file1 file2
hagudu@hagudu-H81M-S1:~/Ethical-Hacking$ ls
file1   file2
hagudu@hagudu-H81M-S1:~/Ethical-Hacking$
```

First we have made directory "Ethical-Hacking". Then we use "cd" to go inside it and, with the help of "ls", we checked that the directory is empty. Afterwards we issue the "touch" command to create two files: "file1" and "file2". Again we issue the "ls" command to check that two files have been created successfully.

In Ethical Hacking, anonymity is a very big deal. In the next chapter we learn it in great detail. Before that you need to understand that, in the process of being anonymous, it is good to be any user rather than the root user. As the root or super user, you first add a user in your virtual Kali Linux. Set a password. Shut down Kali. Reboot and log in as the new user. It is a good practice.

Now how could you add a user? Let us open our virtual Kali and as the root user we'd use the "adduser" command on the terminal. Suppose our new user has a name like "xman". In that case, the command will be very simple: adduser xman.

Once you have issued this command, Kali asks for the password and other details. Give a strong password of at least eight characters with alphanumeric characters. Now shut down your machine and log in as "xman". For other details, it is not mandatory that you need to give your real identity. You can fill them with any data.

As the root or super user you can add as many users as you wish. You can delete them any time. You can restrict their activities from any angle. As an administrator you can add a user who will not be able to log in after six months. You can create groups and set a rule so that entry is restricted. Some users can enter into that group. Some can't.

Primarily you need to add one user, "xman", and log in the system as the new one. A user is not permitted to access or tamper any file of the root or super user. But as super user you can always change the file permission. It is a very important concept from every angle. On the Internet, the concept of file permission is extremely important.

Any file has three types of permissions related to it. It can be only "read only." The meaning is clear. You can't write on it or execute it. It can be "write only." Another state of file is "executable mode." If it is executable, you can perform any action by running it. You can write a simple Python program. This program will take inputs from users and give outputs. After writing a Python file you can make it executable.

Let us see how it happens. Let us open our Kali Linux terminal and, with the help of the "ls" command, we see what we have there presently.

```
sanjib@kali:~$ cd Documents/
sanjib@kali:~/Documents$ ls
VBoxLinuxAdditions.run
sanjib@kali:~/Documents$ ls -la
total 7048
drwxr-xr-x  2 sanjib sanjib     4096 May 29 10:30 .
drwxr-xr-x 18 sanjib sanjib     4096 Jun  3 09:59 ..
-r-xr-xr-x  1 root   root    7208397 May 29 10:30 VBoxLinuxAdditions.run
sanjib@kali:~/Documents$
```

First we go to the "Documents" folder and issue the "ls" command. That shows only one file: "VBoxLinuxAdditions.run". Our next command is "ls –la". It means: we want a listing of all files with all details. You can see the difference above. The output is in red. It shows two hidden files with the previously seen file. And it also shows the owners of files and it also shows the permissions. Let us consider this line minutely.

```
-r-xr-xr-x  1 root    root    7208397 May 29 10:30 VBoxLinuxAdditions.run
```

It tells us that the owner of this file is "root". And the starting line is also very important. It handles file permissions.

```
r-xr-xr-x
```

What does this mean? It has three distinct parts. The first part is "r-x". The second and third parts are also the same: "r-x". The first part is for the owner of the file or current user. The second part is for "group." And the final or third part is for the super user who is viewing this file. I have already created another user, "sanjib", and have logged in as "sanjib". That is why you see this kind of output: sanjib@kali:~/Documents$ ls -la

Now to make this concept more clear we will create a user named "xman". And we will log in as "xman" and see what we have in our Documents folder.

To create a new user, you need to log in as a root or super user. Let us assume we have logged in as "root". The commands and the output are given below.

```
root@kali:~# adduser xman
Adding user `xman' ...
Adding new group `xman' (1002) ...
Adding new user `xman' (1001) with group `xman' ...
Creating home directory `/home/xman' ...
Copying files from `/etc/skel' ...
Enter new UNIX password:
Retype new UNIX password:
passwd: password updated successfully
Changing the user information for xman
Enter the new value, or press ENTER for the default
        Full Name []: xman anonymous
        Room Number []: 123
        Work Phone []: 321
        Home Phone []: 213
        Other []: anon
Is the information correct? [Y/n] y
root@kali:~#
```
Congratulation! You have just successfully created a new user called 'xman'. You notice that it had asked for the password and told you to retype the UNIX password again.

Let us log out as "root" and log in as "xman". Let us also go to the "Documents" folder of "xman" and see what we have.

```
xman@kali:~$ cd Documents/
xman@kali:~/Documents$ ls
xman@kali:~/Documents$ ls -la
total 8
drwxr-xr-x  2 xman xman 4096 Jun  3 10:33 .
drwxr-xr-x 14 xman xman 4096 Jun  3 10:33 ..
```

```
xman@kali:~/Documents$
```

Everything goes as expected. Only one thing is missing. This new user does not have this line: -r-xr-xr-x 1 root root 7208397 May 29 10:30 VBoxLinuxAdditions.run.

Maybe we had moved that executable file from any root folder to the "Documents" folder of user "sanjib" before.

Now we already know how to create a file using "nano" text editor. So we can move on and have a very small Python file. Presumably you don't know Python, so I keep it very simple just to show how we can change file permissions.

```
#!/usr/bin/python3
print("TYpe your name.")
inputs = input(">>>>>>")
outputs = inputs
def main():
    print(outputs)
if __name__ == '__main__':
    main()
```

Inside "nano" editor we write a simple program that will take input and give output. Save the file as "pyfile.py" and exit "nano," and let us issue "ls –la" to see what it shows.

```
xman@kali:~/Documents$ ls -la
total 12
drwxr-xr-x  2 xman xman 4096 Jun  3 10:50 .
drwxr-xr-x 15 xman xman 4096 Jun  3 10:42 ..
-rw-r--r--  1 xman xman   86 Jun  3 10:44 pyfile.py
xman@kali:~/Documents$
```

As you see, the file says everything. It says that now "Documents" folder has one new file, "pyfile.py", and it has been created at 10:44. The owner is "xman" and it has file permissions like this: rw-r--r--

Now you know what this means. It means: the user "xman" can read and write this file but he can't "execute" this file.

```
xman@kali:~/Documents$ chmod +x pyfile.py
xman@kali:~/Documents$ ls -la
total 12
drwxr-xr-x  2 xman xman 4096 Jun  3 10:50 .
drwxr-xr-x 15 xman xman 4096 Jun  3 10:42 ..
-rwxr-xr-x  1 xman xman   86 Jun  3 10:44 pyfile.py
xman@kali:~/Documents$
```

Look how we have used the "chmod" command to change the file permission to executable. Once you have changed the file permission to executable, it changes the color to green. And also look at the file permission: rwxr-xr-x

The first part I mark as red so that you can understand the difference between them. The first part of the permission says "x" has been added since we used the "xman@kali:~/Documents$ chmod +x pyfile.py" command.

Let us execute the file and see how it takes the input and gives the output.

```
xman@kali:~/Documents$ ./pyfile.py
```

Type your name.

```
>>>>>>xman
xman
```

When you run the file, it asks to type your name and gently spits back the output.

Summary

You have learned a few basic Linux commands in this chapter. Now at least you have an idea how a Linux system is working and how you can use your terminal or command line to operate your system.

In the learning process of ethical hacking, you find it extremely useful. In the future, you need to learn few more Linux commands. Your knowledge of Linux or any other operating system must be commendable. As you progress, I hope, your "appetite comes with eating."

We have discussed enough rudiments to stomp our feet on the ground of ethical hacking. Now it is time to move forward. We are ready to take the first important step into the world of ethical hacking by learning a very useful programming language: Python 3.

We have discussed Python 3 in a manner so that you need no programming background. It's been elaborately discussed so that you might reach the intermediate stage and write your own program in Python 3. As you progress in the vast universe of ethical hacking, you'll find the importance of learning Python.

PART II

CHAPTER 6

■ ■ ■

Python 3 and Ethical Hacking

Python can do many things, especially in the socket and networking field. Additionally, in system monitoring it has huge importance. In the advanced level of ethical hacking it can cast a magical spell. You can write your own Python program for any type of security purpose.

Remember, any program written in Python or any language does issue some instructions. And they are more or less same. They are:

INPUT: Get data from keyboard or any file or any source.

OUTPUT: Display data on screen or send it to any file, device or any other source.

MATHEMATICS: Do some basic mathematical operations like add, subtract, multiply or divide. It can be complex also. It depends on your application.

CONDITIONAL EXECUTION: Check that the conditions are properly met. Like "if that is true then do something else/do some other thing."

REPETITION: Perform some action repeatedly.

Most people used to have a Windows or Macintosh platform at their home. Before you start, I ask you to try Linux as a dual operating system. There are a lot of user-friendly, free Linux distributions available. You can try Ubuntu, or any Debian package. Just download the stable ISO image and burn it onto a DVD and install it along with your running OS. It will help. Python comes with every Linux distribution.

The available Linux will run inside Windows so whenever you want to try any open source programming language like Python or PHP, you can take advantage of it. You can try the Linux terminal whenever necessary.

Basically, Python comes with any Linux Distribution, so you need not worry about the installation in Linux. That is also a plus.

If you want to stick to Windows, please visit the download section of the official Python site. According to your system configuration, download the "python-3.4.4.tar.xz" file for windows. When you extract that file, you will get the "python-3.4.4 Windows Installer Package." Just run it and follow the simple steps. I suggest you download the documentation along with the installer package. This documentation is extremely helpful, not only for beginners but for seasoned programmers. After downloading, open the documentation.

© Sanjib Sinha 2017

S. Sinha, *Beginning Ethical Hacking with Python*, DOI 10.1007/978-1-4842-2541-7_6

This documentation is purely designed for programmers, not for beginners. But as a beginner, you need to accustom yourself to this manual so that after a certain period, it becomes a part of your programming life.

Almost every possible programming problem is discussed in this documentation and, moreover, you can develop the code and create some awesome application with the help of this documentation.

It looks like this:

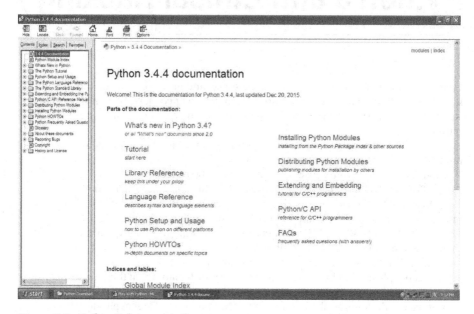

Figure 6-1. *Python 3 documentation page*

CHAPTER 7

■ ■ ■

Python Environment

You are going to learn Python 3. Python 2 has been around for a long time and has a huge library and module support, but Python 3 is the future language. You can also easily install Python 3. Consult the download section of the official web site. In any modern Linux distribution, open your terminal and type "python3". It will give you the Python interpreter or shell where you can write your code.

Remember, Python comes with every modern Linux distribution. So you need not install it anymore. But a few packages you might need to install. There are tons of tutorials and a lot of community help you can get over the Internet.

The Python interpreter on a typical Linux distribution looks like this:

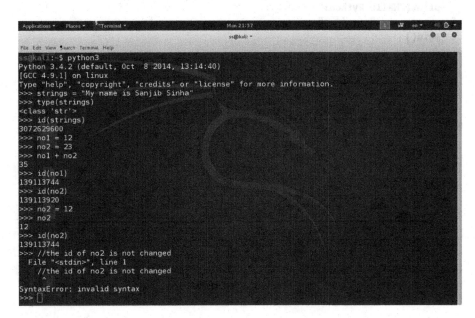

Figure 7-1. *Image of Python interpreter*

In any modern Linux distribution, you need not do anything. Open the terminal and type "python3", and you will have an output like this:

```
hagudu@hagudu-H81M-S1:~$ python3
Python 3.4.3 (default, Oct 14 2015, 20:28:29)
[GCC 4.8.4] on linux
Type "help", "copyright", "credits" or "license" for more information.
>>>
```

It says my computer has Python 3.4.3. Now you can write some code directly on it to get some output like this:

```
>>> name = "Sanjib"
>>> print(name)
Sanjib
>>>
```

In Linux, you save a Python file first. Write this code:

```
<code>
#!/usr/bin/python3
def main():
    print("Hello Python!")
if __name__ == "__main__":
    main()
</code>
```

If you are new to Linux, first save this Python file as "hello.py" and then change it to executable with this command:

```
sudo chmod +x hello.py
```

On the terminal, run this file with this command:

```
./hello.py
```

It will give the output: **Hello Python!**

This is your first Python code.

For Windows, download Python installer and document. The document comes in a ".chm" file. It will help later. To install Python, just run the installer. It will be installed in your "C" drive in a minute. Now you can go to "all programs" and run Python from there. Normally, a small IDE called IDLE comes with Python. You can write code and just run it. Let us see how it looks:

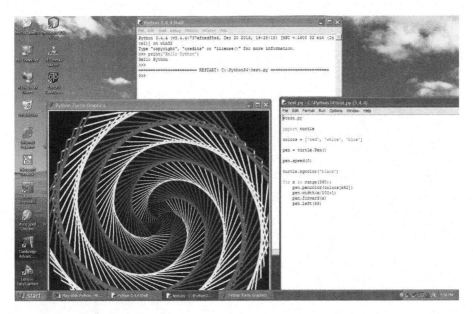

Figure 7-2. Python IDE in Windows

In the above image, you see on the top is IDLE, which is the Python Shell. You can directly get output from it. You can also go the file section of IDLE and create a new file. I have done that. I created a file, "test.py", and wrote some code in it. Then from IDLE you can either run this module or just press F5 and it will keep running. As you see in the picture, our Python code drew a beautiful shape. In Windows 7 or later, you can open Power Shell and type the same thing and you will get the same result. But I prefer you install a good Python text editor or IDE first.

For Linux, "Pycharm" community edition is a good choice. It is free. For Windows or Mac, there are several good free text editors. Search on the Internet and install. The main advantage is you don't have to indent every line of code. It is automated. Second, the support of a large Python library is available in every IDE.

CHAPTER 8

General Syntaxes

In this chapter we will learn something just to try some codes. We will learn the same things in detail later. All we need to do now is just try to write some code in Python and see how it works. At the same time, we will learn about the general syntaxes used often in Python.

Create the main( ) function

As I said, Python scripts are almost like human language. You need not use a lot of special characters or symbols. All you need to remember is that "indentation" plays a very important role in Python. When you apply some special conditions inside your code, this indentation is important.

Few things repeat in every code. So you can write it out in a separate file and just use them in every new Python file. The general syntax structure code looks like this:

```
<code>
#!/usr/bin/python3
def main():
    print("I am a general syntax Python file")
if __name__ == "__main__":
    main()
</code>
```

Save this file as "general-syntax.py". When you execute this file, it will say or print out: "I am a general syntax Python file."

The very first line, "*#!/usr/bin/python3*", denotes the path of Python interpreter. The greatness of Python is that it remains same in every operating system. In the second part we have defined a main() function and, under that main() function, we can call any function. Without a main() function, you cannot call a function before it is defined. Consider this example:

```
<code>
#!/usr/bin/python3
def main():
    print("I am a general syntax Python file")
    LetUsDoSomething()
```

© Sanjib Sinha 2017
S. Sinha, *Beginning Ethical Hacking with Python*, DOI 10.1007/978-1-4842-2541-7_8

```
def LetUsDoSomething():
    print("I am doing something")

if __name__ == "__main__":
    main()
</code>
```

Now it will give a nice output like this:

I am a general syntax Python file
I am doing something

Suppose you don't have any main() function. Now if you want to call the function LetUsDoSomething() before that function is defined, it will give an error.

Try this code and see the error:

```
<code>
#!/usr/bin/python3
LetUsDoSomething()
def LetUsDoSomething():
    print("I am doing something")
</code>
```

It says: NameError LetUsDoSomething() is not defined. You can always call it after the function is defined. In that case, you don't need the main() function defined. But in a long line of code where many functions are involved, it is not always possible to maintain it. To solve that problem, it is a good practice to define the main() function first. After that you can write any function after the main() function and call it inside the main().

Indentation and White Space

They play a very vital role when you work with Python.

Indentation or white space is very, very important. Before you start learning Python, you need to understand this properly. Consider this code:

```
<code>
# coding=utf-8
def main():
    print('A line inside main function.')
print("A line outside main function.")
if __name__ == main():main()
</code>
```

Look at this code. The print() function inside the main() function has been indented. It has about four spaces. And the second print() function is outside the main() function. And look at the code; it falls on the same line with the main() function. So when we run this program, the outside print() function executes first. And the output is like this:

```
//output
A line outside main function.
A line inside main function.
//output ended
```

If we try to push the outside print() function a little bit inside, it will give an error, because Python interpreter will think that it is inside the main() function. Actually this is not true. If we want to push that "outside print() function" inside the main() function, we need to place it on the same line of the inside print() function like this:

```
<code>
# coding=utf-8
def main():
    print('A line inside main function.')
    print("A line outside main function.")
if __name__ == main():main()
</code>
```

Now the output changes. It looks like this:

```
//output
A line inside main function.
A line outside main function.
//output ended
```

We learn a very important lesson that we should learn by heart. The lesson is: white space or indentation in Python plays a major role. When we write a function and put some other functions inside it, they must fall on the same line. In any text editor or IDE, it is automatically done. When you press the "enter" or "return" key, the following lines keep falling on the same line. If you want to go outside that function, just follow the first example. Just to understand how indentation works in Python, we write a little lengthy code and see how it looks.

```
<code>
# coding=utf-8
def main():
    # print('A line inside main function.')
    #
    # print("A line outside main function.")
    OutsideMainFunction()
```

45

```
def OutsideMainFunction():
    x = 0
    while x < 5:
        print(x)
        x = x + 1
if __name__ == main():main()
</code>
```

Look at the code. We have a main() function. Additionally, we have a function called "OutsideMainFunction()'". It is really outside of the main() function. So they are different functions and they have their own indentations. Inside of the "OutsideMainFunction()" we see a "while loop." That "while loop" also has its own indentation. Actually we better call it "block." So every block of code has its own "white space" or the code inside that block is indented accordingly. If you don't use any IDE and try to write it on your terminal, you have to use the space bar. Inside a function, if you use "four spaces," then whatever you write inside that function must fall on the same line. That is, whenever you write a new line, it must have "four spaces." You cannot give two or three space suddenly. But if you write another function, you can change that rule. In that case, the new function has its own block of code and it has its own rule. You may use two spaces now.

Commenting

In any kind of programming, commenting is very important. Another programmer will read your program. Your every step should be readable. If there is any kind of twist or you try something special, you must explain that inside your code. Consider this code:

```
<code>
# this is main() function
def main():
    OutsideMainFunction()
# this function is outside main() function
def OutsideMainFunction():
    x = 0
    while x < 5:
        print(x)
        x = x + 1
if __name__ == main():main()
</code>
```

Normally any comment is written with a # (hash) mark. When Python interpreter sees #, it knows that is a comment and it ignores it. In our code, we clearly define what is the main() function and we also say in our comments that there is another function which is outside the main() function.

Normally a seasoned programmer never comments such simple stuff. But to begin with, you can add comments when you feel it is necessary. Because after some time, when you revisit your old codes, you can remember why you did that. Commenting is useful in that way. At the same time, you cannot trust all comments. Programmers often forget to change comments when they change their codes.

Assigning Values

In Python, the assignment operator is an equal (=) sign. When you write "a = 10", it means "a" is a variable or a container. This variable "a" is assigned to an integer value. What is that value? It is 10. This value could have been a string. What is a string? A string is an addition of characters. Suppose you write "b = Two". It means the variable "b" is assigned to a string value, and that string is "Two", which is nothing more than three characters: "T"+"w"+"o". According to your assignment, Python interprets the value and keeps a definite storage place for them. It knows how many bits and bytes will be required for them.

In Python, everything is object. Python is an object-oriented programming language. As a beginner, you may not understand this concept. Don't worry. We will discuss it in detail as we progress. You will learn it. Presently you just remember that an object means an instance of class. Imagine yourself as an object. In that case, you are an instance of "human" class. You have some properties like height, width, etc. You also can do something. The "human" class is a blueprint of you and other humans and in "human" class, everything has been well-defined. There are a lot of properties and a lot of action verbs defined. And according to that definition, you, me, and other humans keep doing things.

When we say in Python that everything is an object, it means everything has a class or blueprint behind it. We write like this:

```
<code>
#!/usr/bin/python3
# coding=utf-8
a = 1
print(a)
print(type(a))
print(id(a))
a = "One"
print(a)
print(type(a))
print(id(a))
</code>
```

And the output is like this:

```
//output
1
<class 'int'>
139113568
One
<class 'str'>
3073583584
//output ended
```

In the next chapter we will learn about it in more detail.

CHAPTER 9

■ ■ ■

Variables, Objects and Values

In Python everything is an object. To start with, you need to remember a few things:

1. **Variables, functions and even code are objects.**

2. **Every object has an ID, type, and value.**

    ID stands for identification of a particular instance of an object. This ID cannot change in the lifetime of that object.

3. **Type identifies a class of an object. It cannot change for the life of object.**

4. **Value is the content of the object and mutable objects can only change value. Immutable objects cannot change value.**

5. **Every variable in Python is a first class object. What looks like a simple variable actually is something more complex.**

Let us see what these terms mean.

```
<code>
#!/usr/bin/python3
def main():
    x = 1
    print(x)
    print(id(x))
    print(type(x))
    x = 2
    print(x)
    print(id(x))
    print(type(x))
    x = 1
    print(x)
    print(id(x))
    print(type(x))
```

© Sanjib Sinha 2017

S. Sinha, *Beginning Ethical Hacking with Python*, DOI 10.1007/978-1-4842-2541-7_9

```
if __name__ == "__main__":
    main()
</code>
```

Here is the output:

```
<blockquote>
1
10455040
class 'int'
2
10455072
class 'int'
1
10455040
class 'int'
</blockquote>
```

As you see, changing values of "x" does not affect the immutable objects and the unique identifier of object "1" remains same. What has been changed is simply the reference of the variable. First, we referred "1" (immutable integer object) to "x" (variable), and then change it. The ID and type remain same.

Remember, numbers, strings, and "tuples" are immutable. Lists, dictionaries, and other objects are mutable (changeable), but it depends.

Let us see a very brief example where it is explained in the comment section. The output is given along with it.

```
<code>
#!/usr/bin/python3
# in python everything is object
# a variable is a reference to an object
# each object has an identity or an ID
x = 1
print(type(x))
print(id(x))
##################
# class 'int'
# 139113568
##################
# number, string, tuple -> immutable
# list, dictionary -> mutable
x = 1
y = 1
print(type(x))
print(id(x))
print(type(y))
print(id(y))
```

```
if x == y:
    print("True")
else:
    print("False")
if x is y:
    print("True")
else:
    print("False")
################
# see the last two lines, both are true
# class 'int'
# 139113568
# class 'int'
# 139113568
# True
# True
################
a = dict(x = 1, y = 1)
print(type(a))
print(id(a))
b = dict(x = 1, y = 1)
print(id(b))
if a == b:
    print("True")
else:
    print("False")
if a is b:
    print("True")
else:
    print("False")
################
    # see the last two lines, one is true but the id is not same so it is
false
# class 'dict'
# 3072650252
# 3072692524
# True
# False
################
for i in range(0, 3):
    print(i, "=", id(i))
################
# 0 = 139113552
# 1 = 139113568
# 2 = 139113584
################
</code>
```

We see the output inside the code. You notice that every output is commented out so that when we run this code, it will never affect the main script. There are a lot of values. Integers, strings, tuples, lists, and finally dictionaries.

Now we will understand what they actually are and how they work.

Using Numbers

In Python there are two kinds of numbers. One is an integer and the other is a float. We have built-in methods in Python that can change an integer to a float and change a float to an integer. I hope you will understand the code below. The output is self-explanatory. Read the comment also.

```python
<code>
#!/usr/bin/python3
def main():
    x = 3
    print(x)
    print(id(x))
    print(type(x))
    print("********")
    x = 3 /2
    print(x)
    print(id(x))
    print(type(x))
    print("********")
    x = round(42 / 9)
    print(x)
    print(id(x))
    print(type(x))
    print("********")
    # we want to round it up
    x = 42 // 9
    print(x)
    print(id(x))
    print(type(x))
    print("********")
    # how many digits we want to round to
    x = round(42 / 9, 3)
    print(x)
    print(id(x))
    print(type(x))
    print("********")
    x = 43 % 7
    print(x)
    print(id(x))
    print(type(x))
    print("********")
    x = int(34.78)
```

```
    print(x)
    print(id(x))
    print(type(x))
    print("********")
    x = float(23)
    print(x)
    print(id(x))
    print(type(x))
    print("********")
if __name__ == "__main__":
    main()
</code>
```

And here is the output we get from this code:

```
<blockquote>
3
10455104
class 'int'
********
1.5
140223146811728
class 'float'
********
4
10455136
class 'int'
********
5
140223146823568
class 'int'
********
4.667
140223146811968
class 'float'
********
1
10455040
class 'int'
********
34
10456096
class 'int'
********
23.0
140223146811968
class 'float'
********
</blockquote>
```

As you see in the output, each number has a class and an ID. For numbers, this ID is immutable. So if you assign the same number (suppose it is 1) to two different variables, like this: a = 1 and b = 1; the ID of "a" and "b" is the same.

String

In Python string is an immutable object and can be written within double quotes or single quotes. Consider this code:

```
<code>
#!/usr/bin/python3
def main():
    strings = "I love you."
    print(strings)
    anotherStrings = "I love you but\nI don't know how much you love me."
    print(anotherStrings)
if __name__ == "__main__":
    main()
</code>
```

And here is the output:

```
<blockquote>
I love you.
I love you but
I don't know how much you love me.
</blockquote>
```

As you see, we used a backslash to get a new line. And we got an exact break where we needed it.

There is also raw string output. See this code:

```
<code>
#!/usr/bin/python3
def main():
    strings = "I love you."
    print(strings)
    anotherStrings = "I love you but\nI don't know how much you love me."
    print(anotherStrings)
    rawStrings = r"I love you but\nI don't know how much you love me."
    print(rawStrings)
if __name__ == "__main__":
    main()
</code>
```

And here is the output:

```
<blockquote>
I love you.
I love you but
I don't know how much you love me.
I love you but\nI don't know how much you love me.
</blockquote>
```

The last statement is called a raw string, where a backslash is not working anymore and we get a raw output. And it is used in regular expression. We will discuss it in detail in our regular expression chapter.

We can insert an integer into the middle of a string. I show you both the methods used in Python 2 and Python 3 but remember, you better stick to the construct used in Python 3.

Let us first see the Python 2 code:

```
<code>
days = 8
lyrics = "%s days a week is not enough to love you." %days
print(lyrics)
</code>
```

The output is like this:

```
<blockquote>
8 days a week is not enough to love you.
</blockquote>
```

Let us now see the Python 3 code:

```
<code>
days = 8
lyrics = "{} days a week is not enough to love you."
print(lyrics.format(days))
</code>
```

The output:

```
<blockquote>
8 days a week is not enough to love you.
</blockquote>
```

What is the major difference between these two constructs? The difference is in the latest version of Python; we treat string as an object. Hence a "lyrics" object used a method called format() and passed a parameter that it wanted to format into it. In the line print(lyrics.format(days)) we used a period ("."), to call the method format() which is built-in in the string class.

In your coding life you need to use plenty of strings and some of them might have multiple line breaks. You cannot use backslash "n" each time. It is cumbersome.

There is a trick you can use in Python to use multiple new lines.

```
<code>
newLines = """\
first line
second line
third line
more to come...
"""
print(newLines)
</code>
```

In the output the lines break up automatically.

```
<blockquote>
first line
second line
third line
more to come...
</blockquote>
```

Now you can use single quote instead of double quotes. You can use no backslash at the beginning, but that will generate a space in the beginning of the line.

What is Type and ID

Python is an object-oriented programming language. Everything is an object here. Every object has a unique identification, which is known as ID. Let us open our terminal in Linux or, if you have Windows or Mac, open the Python Shell and test this code:

```
<code>

>>> x = 10
>>> x
10
>>> type(x)
<class 'int'>
>>> id(x)
10455328

>>> y = 10

>>> y
```

```
10
>>> type(y)
<class 'int'>
>>> id(y)
10455328
>>> a = dict(name='sanjib')
>>> a
{'name': 'sanjib'}
>>> type(a)
<class 'dict'>
>>> id(a)
139984318683592
>>> b = dict(name='sanjib')
>>> b
{'name': 'sanjib'}
>>> type(b)
<class 'dict'>
>>> id(b)
139984318683720
>>> a == b
True
>>> a is b
False
>>>
```

Here we first assign an integer value "10" to the variable "x" and later assign the same value to "y". Later we check the ID of two variables and found that the ID is the same. We said this in the previous section. Now you see the output.

We can check whether two objects assigned to two different variables is the same or not by writing this way:

```
<code>
>>> x == y

True

>>> x is y

True
>>>
</code>
```

Here it is evident that both the variables "x" and "y" are pointed to the same integer object, "10". So the value is same and the variables are also same. But it did not happen in case of a dictionary object that we had written just after that. The dictionary "a" and "b" have the same value, but since dictionary objects are mutable, it changes the ID.

```
<code>
>>> a = dict(name='sanjib')

>>> a

{'name': 'sanjib'}

>>> type(a)

<class 'dict'>

>>> id(a)

139984318683592

>>> b = dict(name='sanjib')

>>> b

{'name': 'sanjib'}

>>> type(b)

<class 'dict'>

>>> id(b)
```

```
139984318683720

>>> a == b

True

>>> a is b

False

>>>
<code>
```

It says the dictionary ID changes, though two variables have same values. When we check it logically, it says, yes, the value of two variables is same, but since the ID is different they are different objects.

As a beginner, you may find this concept a little bit strange. But later, as you progress, you will find this concept is extremely helpful. A dictionary object needs to be changed for programming purposes. If two dictionary objects have same ID, we cannot change them.

Logical Values

Let us consider another shell script for testing logical values: True and False.

```
<code>
>>> a, b = 0, 1

>>> a == b

False

>>> a < b

True

>>> a > b

False

>>> a = True

>>> a

True

>>> type(a)
```

```
<class 'bool'>

>>> id(a)

10348608

>>> b = True

>>> b

True

>>> type(b)

<class 'bool'>

>>> id(b)

10348608

>>>
```
</code>

Here we see there are "bool" classes and the "==" operator represents the test for quality between two values. Since "a" has a value of 0 and "b" has value of 1, the output is "False". Is "a" less than "b"? Yes. So the output comes out as "True".

These "True" and "False" represent "bool" classes. And it is "immutable", so if two variables are both "True" they have same ID.

Tuples And Lists.

Python has many sequential types (lists of things). Let us consider this code:

```
<code>
x = (1, 2, 3, 4)
print(x)
print(type(x))
</code>
```

It has output like this:

```
<blockquote>
(1, 2, 3, 4)
class 'tuple'
</blockquote>
```

So it is of the class "tuple" and it has a list of things. Remember, tuple is immutable. You cannot insert or update it. But you can iterate through it like this:

```
for i in x:
    print(i)
```

It will give all the numbers you have inside the tuple.

On the contrary, "list" is another sequential type that is mutable and you can change it as necessary. Consider this code:

```
a = [1, 2, 3, 4]
print(a)
print(type(a))
```

It has output like this:

> [1, 2, 3, 4]
> class 'list'

You can insert or update it as you need. Suppose you want to append the "tuple x" in this list and you also want to insert the "tuple x" in the beginning. So the full code looks like this:

```
#!/usr/bin/python3
# tuple
x = (1, 2, 3, 4)

# list
a = [1, 2, 3, 4]

# appending tuple x to list
a.append(x)
print(a)

# inserting tuple x in the first position
a.insert(0, x)
print(a)

# Now iterating the final list a
for i in a:
    print(i)
```

And the output is like this:

<blockquote>
```
[1, 2, 3, 4, (1, 2, 3, 4)] # after appending
[(1, 2, 3, 4), 1, 2, 3, 4, (1, 2, 3, 4)] # after inserting
# When we iterate the list 'a' the output looks like this
(1, 2, 3, 4)
1
2
3
4
(1, 2, 3, 4)
```
</blockquote>

In Python, a string is also a sequential type and you can iterate through it. Consider this code:

<code>
```
strings = "This is a string."
for WeWillIterateThroughIt in strings:
    print(WeWillIterateThroughIt)
```
</code>

And the output is as usual:

<blockquote>
```
T
h
i
s

i
s

a

s
t
r
i
n
g
.
```
</blockquote>

A string is a sequential type. Consider this code:

```
strings = "string."
print(strings[1:3])
```

It means the string goes like this:

```
0 = s
1 = t
2 = r
3 = i
4 = n
5 = g
```

So **strings[1:3]** means the sequence starts from position 1 and it goes up to position 3, excluding the 3rd position. It means it stops at 2nd position. So the output is as expected:

> **tr**

Dictionary

Python has another very strong aggregate type of values: dictionary. It is a class, as usual. It is more like associative array or hash in other languages.

Consider this code:

```
#!usr/bin/python3
EnglishDictionaries = {'bare':'jejune', 'anger':'dudgeon',
'abuse':'vituperate', 'howl':'ululate'}
print(EnglishDictionaries)
# getting in a nmore human readable form
for keys in EnglishDictionaries:
    print(keys, "=", EnglishDictionaries[keys])
```

And the output is:

> {'abuse': 'vituperate', 'bare': 'jejune', 'howl': 'ululate', 'anger': 'dudgeon'}

```
abuse = vituperate
bare = jejune
howl = ululate
anger = dudgeon
</blockquote>
```

Now we can sort this dictionary in an alphabetical order like this:

```
<code>
EnglishDictionaries = {'bare':'jejune', 'anger':'dudgeon',
'abuse':'vituperate', 'howl':'ululate'}
for keys in sorted(EnglishDictionaries.keys()):
    print(keys, "=", EnglishDictionaries[keys])
</code>
```

And we get a nice clean output in alphabetical order:

```
<blockquote>
abuse = vituperate
anger = dudgeon
bare = jejune
howl = ululate
</blockquote>
```

We can also write dictionary another way using a construct of the class dictionary. Consider this code:

```
<code>
synonyms = dict(bare='jejune', anger='dudgeon', abuse= 'vituperate', howl=
'ululate')
</code>
```

We have just changed the variable name but used the same pair of words. Now we can sort them as before to get the same result. Remember one thing: when you use dict() function, you should not write keys within quotes but string values should be quoted like I did. Since dictionary is mutable, you can insert key value pairs into it, like lists.

Object

Python is an object-oriented language. We will discuss it later in detail. Let us say there is a class or blueprint and from this class or blueprint we can get many types of objects. Take Human class. It is a very complex class indeed! It has many kinds of properties; many kinds of actions are performed by this class. When we create an object or instance of this class, this object or instance can carry forward every single trait of this class. Remember, there has always been a good human being and a bad human being.

Let us assume a Human class has two types of humans: one is good and the other is bad. In reality, it is not so simple. But to begin with our learning, we start with a less complex scenario.

Consider the code below:

```python
<code>
#!/usr/bin/python3
class Human:
    def __init__(self, kind = "Good"):
        self.kind = kind
    def whatKind(self):
        return self.kind
def main():
    GoodHuman = Human()
    print(GoodHuman.whatKind())
    BadHuman = Human("Bad")
    print(BadHuman.whatKind())
if __name__ == "__main__":
    main()
</code>
```

And here is the output:

```
<blockquote>
Good
Bad
</blockquote>
```

In the above code the object is the instance of a class and encapsulates every property and method of the class or blueprint. In the above class, we assume a sort of blueprint where every human being is good. So in the initialization method, we write this code:

```python
<code>
class Human:
    def __init__(self, kind = "Good"):
        self.kind = kind
    def whatKind(self):
        return self.kind
</code>
```

Here, "self" means a reference to the object. And the next parameter defines the kind of human objects we want to create.

What does this line mean?

```python
<code>
def whatKind(self):
        return self.kind
</code>
```

65

It returns the value of what kind of human object we want to create. The next steps are quite self-explanatory as it goes:

```
<code>
def main():
    GoodHuman = Human()
    print(GoodHuman.whatKind())
    BadHuman = Human("Bad")
    print(BadHuman.whatKind())
if __name__ == "__main__":
    main()
</code>
```

When we create our first object, "GoodHuman", we need not pass any value as "good" as the default value that has already been passed implicitly through the initialization process. But when we want to create "BadHuman", we need to pass the value explicitly and it returns that value.

CHAPTER 10

Conditionals

In Python there are two types of conditionals. They are: conditional executions and conditional values or conditional expressions. In conditional executions we execute or check the condition of the statement. We know that between two values there could be three types of conditions. It is either less than or greater than or it is equal. Write this code:

```
<code>
def conditionals_exec():
    a, b = 1, 3
    if a < b:
        print("a is less than b")
    elif a > b:
        print("a is greater than b")
    else:
        print("a is equal to b")
conditionals_exec()

</code>
```

The output is:

```
#######################
# a is less than b
#######################
```

The output is obvious. Now you can change the value and test the code. Now try to rewrite the above statement in a different way. We can say x is either less than y or greater than y. Otherwise, it is obvious that they are equal.

```
<code>
def conditional_values():
    a, b = 1, 2
    statements = "less than " if a < b else " not less than."
    print(statements)
conditional_values()
</code>
```

© Sanjib Sinha 2017

S. Sinha, *Beginning Ethical Hacking with Python*, DOI 10.1007/978-1-4842-2541-7_10

These functions can be written more conveniently and neatly with the main() functions now:

```
<code>

def main():
    print("This is main function.")
    conditionals_exec()
    conditional_values()

def conditionals_exec():
    a, b = 1, 3
    if a < b:
        print("a is less than b")
    elif a > b:
        print("a is greater than b")
    else:
        print("a is equal to b")

def conditional_values():
    a, b = 1, 2
    statements = "less than " if a < b else " not less than."
    print(statements)

if __name__ == "__main__": main()

</code>
```

If we run this program now, the output will be:

```
########################
# This is main function.
# less than
# a is less than b
########################
```

Now we can change the place of conditional_values(), and conditionals_exec() and the output will change accordingly:

```
########################
# This is main function.
# a is less than b
# less than
########################
```

CHAPTER 11

Loops

"While loop" is the simplest form of loop in Python. But you need to understand it properly. Otherwise it can end up eating up your memory running the infinity loop. Usually most of the jobs are done by "for loop". But in some special cases, you need to use "while loop". A basic understanding is important.

While Loops

In plain English we often say, "While it is true it keeps on running. While it is not true it stops." Logically, the same thing happens here. While a statement is true, the process is going on. You need a mechanism to stop that process. That is important. Otherwise that statement will eat up your memory.

Consider this code:

```
<code>
b = 1
while b < 50:
    print(b)
    b = b + 1
</code>
```

What does it mean? It means, the statement "b < 50" is true until the suite or block of code is true inside it. Inside the block we wrote "b = b + 1" and before the beginning of the while loop we defined the value of b as 1.

So in each step b progresses by adding 1 to its value and finishes at 49. In the output you will get 1 to 49.

Let us move further. Consider this code:

```
<code>
#!/usr/bin/python3
# simple fibonacci series
# sum of two numbers define the next set
a, b = 0, 1
while b < 50:
    print(b, end=' ')
    a, b = b, a + b
</code>
```

© Sanjib Sinha 2017
S. Sinha, *Beginning Ethical Hacking with Python*, DOI 10.1007/978-1-4842-2541-7_11

The output is quite obvious:

<blockquote>
1 1 2 3 5 8 13 21 34
</blockquote>

For the beginners, let us write this code in a more readable way and it will give a different output altogether:

<code>
```
#!/usr/bin/python3
a, b = 0, 1
while b < 30:
    print(b, end=' ')
    a = b
    b = a + b
```
</code>

Let us explain the steps one by one to understand it properly.

The loop starts with 1. In the first step, the value of "a" is 1. In the next step value of "b" is 2. Now the value of "a" is 2 so the value of "b" is 4. Now the value of "a" is 4 so the value of "b" is 8 (4+4). Now the value of "a" is 8 so the value of "b" is (8 + 8) = 16. Now the value of "a" is 16. What will be the value of b? It will be 16 + 16 = 32. But 32 is greater than 30. So it will come out from the code suite of the while loop.

The output of the above code will be:

<blockquote>
1 2 4 8 16
</blockquote>

Let us write the whole bunch of code in a new format:

<code>
```
#!/usr/bin/python3
# simple fibonacci series
# sum of two numbers define the next set
a, b = 0, 1
while b < 30:
    print("a = ", a, "=" , "b = ", b, "," , end=' ')
    a, b = b, a + b
print("**********")
a, b = 0, 1
while b < 30:
    print("a = ", a, "=" , "b = ", b, "," , end=' ')
    a = b
    b = a + b
```
</code>

And the output will be:

```
<blockquote>
a =  0 and b =  1 , a =  1 and b =  1 , a =  1 and b =  2 , a =  2 and b =
3 , a =  3 and b =  5 , a =  5 and b =  8 , a =  8 and b =  13 , a =  13 and
b =  21 ,
********** Lines of separation **********
a =  0 and b =  1 , a =  1 and b =  2 , a =  2 and b =  4 , a =  4 and b =
8 , a =  8 and b =  16 ,
</blockquote>
```

Now hopefully, this explains how the while loops work.

For Loops

The most common loop used in Python is for loop. In fact, essentially almost all kinds of looping jobs can be done through the "for" loop.

There is a reason of course. With the help of for loop, we can iterate through Python objects and we can iterate through most of the Python objects. Let us see one example:

```
<code>
#!/usr/bin/python3
songs = open('file.txt')
for lines in songs.read():
    print(lines, end='')
</code>
```

And the output of the song goes like this:

```
<blockquote>
Yo, girl you touched me hard
your loneliness has made me weep
I am a sooo stupid nerd
I thought about the words, I could not keep
So I weep
A stupid nerd
</blockquote>
```

We have a song written over in a file called "file.txt" and we just iterate through this file. We could have iterated through line by line as they are indexed. Consider this code where we just used "enumerate()" function and **index value**:

```
<code>
# enumerate
songs = open('file.txt')
for index, lines in enumerate(songs.readlines()):
    print(index, lines, end='')
</cede>
```

And the output is like this:

```
<blockquote>
0 Yo, girl you touched me hard
1 your loneliness has made me weep
2 I am a sooo stupid nerd
3 I thought about the words, I could not keep
4 So I weep
5 A stupid nerd
</blockquote>
```

Now what does this function "enumerate()" mean? Dictionary says: enumeration is a kind of numbering which is a numbered list. Let us consider this line of code:

```
<code>
strings = "This is a string."
# now we are going to find how many 's' is inside this string
for index, s in enumerate(strings):
    if s == 's':
        print("Hi I am 's' and I am located at position {}".format(index))
</code>
```

And we have an output:

```
<blockquote>
Hi I am 's' and I am located at position 3
Hi I am 's' and I am located at position 6
Hi I am 's' and I am located at position 10
</blockquote>
```

This is extremely useful. You can search any character inside any string. In Python, functions or subroutines are extremely important for reusability of codes. We can call a function for several times and pass many arguments or parameters to get different effects. Now we are going to pass one parameter inside the loops() function. Consider this code below:

```
<code>
#!/usr/bin/python3
def main():
    loops(0)
    loops()
    loops(3)
```

```
def loops(a = 4):
    for i in range(a, 6):
        print(i, " ")
    print("*************")
if __name__ == "__main__":
    main()
</code>
```

What does this code mean? In loops() function, we have passed one parameter a and assigned a value 4. It is the default value. So that in the future if we forget to pass any argument the code will not break.

We have called that function three times inside main() function, but with three different values, and one of them is NULL. That is, we have not passed any argument.

The output changes with the new code:

```
<blockquote>
0
1
2
3
4
5
*************
4
5
*************
3
4
5
*************
</blockquote>
```

Now it is obvious that you can play around with this code. You can pass two arguments inside loops() function and control the range() function to get different values.

CHAPTER 12

Regular Expressions

Searching and replacing with regular expressions is equally easy and very simple in nature. To do that we will tweak our old code a little bit. We use "re" module and it does the simple jobs. Regular expression is itself a big topic. We try to understand the basic things so that we can use it in our future projects.

Using "re" Module

If you want to use "re" module, the first step is importation. We need to import the module first and write it on the top of the code. Consider this code where we have a text file called "file.txt" and it is stored in our "primary" folder.

```
<code>
#!/usr/bin/python3
import re
def main():
    ReplaceWord()
    DEmarcationLine()
    MatchAndReplaceWord()

def ReplaceWord():
    try:
        files = open("../primary/file.txt")
        for line in files:
            # you can search any word
            print(re.sub('lenor|more', "#####", line), end=' ')
    except FileNotFoundError as e:
        print("File was not found:", e)

def MatchAndReplaceWord():
    try:
        files = open("../primary/file.txt")
        for line in files:
            # you can search any pattern that can match and then replace
            with this word
```

© Sanjib Sinha 2017
S. Sinha, *Beginning Ethical Hacking with Python*, DOI 10.1007/978-1-4842-2541-7_12

```
            match = re.search('(len|neverm)ore', line)
            if match:
                print(line.replace(match.group(), "#####"), end=' ')
    except FileNotFoundError as e:
        print("File was not found:", e)

def DEmarcationLine():
    print("*************")

if __name__ == "__main__":
    main()
</code>
```

Before we have the output, let us see what is written inside the file. The "file.txt" in "primary" folder has these lines:

```
<blockquote>
first line lenore
it is nine, second line and dine
third line and nevermore over
and fourth
fifth pine line lenore
and the tremor
here is more line
and a new line
i love you
where you are staying now?
i don't know
</blockquote>
```

As you see, these are not very meaningful sentences. Our primary concern is very simple. We write down some nonsense lines and later try to work upon it with the use of "re" module. Now we run the code and here is the output:

```
<blockquote>
first line #####e
 it is nine, second line and dine
 third line and never##### over
 and fourth
 fifth pine line #####e
 and the tremor
 here is ##### line
 and a new line
 i love you
 where you are staying now?
 i don't know *************
```

```
first line #####
 third line and ##### over
 fifth pine line #####
</blockquote>
```

All the words "lenore" and "nevermore" have been replaced by five hashtags: "#####". We use two methods of "re" module that we import and write on the top of the code. These methods are "re.sub()" and "line.replace()". We have supplied the old string and the new word. We have given five hashtags but you could have given any other word, of course.

Reusing With Regular Expressions

You have already seen how we can search and replace words in a file with the help of regular expression. Now we will try to reuse the code so that we can use them again and again. Additionally, we will also try to write them in a more readable way.

Let us first write the steps. What we want to achieve is very important. Let us have a clear idea first and the best way is writing it down.

1. We need to open a file and put it into the "try block" to avoid getting any nasty error message. Beginners may find this "try block" quite intimidating. I have not explained it before and suddenly started using it. I have done it intentionally. It is explained in the next chapter, "Exceptions, Catching Errors." But before that, I want you to write them and get habituated to a concept that looks complex. Once you learn this "try block," please revisit this code again. You will find it extremely easy! Moreover, as you progress, you will find that using "try block" is always a good habit.

2. Get the pattern of the words that we want to search and, using flags, we can ignore case.

3. Use that "re" module search method to see if that pattern matches with our line.

4. Now if it matches, then replace it with new words.

Consider this code below and read the comments. In comments I briefly explain what I am going to do.

```
<code>
#!/usr/bin/python3
import re

def main():
```

```
        CompilerAndReplaceWord()

def CompilerAndReplaceWord():
    try:
        files = open("../primary/file.txt")
        # you can search any pattern that can match ignoring the upper or
        lower case
        pattern = re.compile('(len|neverm)ore', re.IGNORECASE)
        for line in files:
            # re module search that pattern in a line
            if re.search(pattern, line):
                # we found that patetrn and now it is time to replace them
with a new string
                print(pattern.sub("######", line), end=' ')
    except FileNotFoundError as e:
        print("File was not found:", e)

if __name__ == "__main__":
    main()
</code>
```

And in the output it replaces all the words "lenore" and "nevermore" with six hashtags. To do that, it also checks the upper and lower case and finally replaces them all.

```
<blockquote>
first line ######
 third line and ###### over
 fifth pine line ######
 i don't know ######
</blockquote>
```

Searching with Regular Expressions

Regular expressions are a very powerful method of matching patterns. Regular expression is a small language in itself and it can be very simple and very complex.

It is implemented in Python with "re" module.

Consider this code:

```
<code>
#!/usr/bin/python3
import re
def main():
    FindWord()
    DEmarcationLine()
    MatchWord()
def FindWord():
    try:
```

```
        files = open("../primary/file.txt")
        for line in files:
            # you can search any word
            if re.search('lenor|more', line):
                print(line, end=' ')
    except FileNotFoundError as e:
        print("Fiel was not found:", e)
def MatchWord():
    try:
        files = open("../primary/file.txt")
        for line in files:
            # you can search any pattern that can match this word
            match = re.search('(len|neverm)ore', line)
            if match:
                print(match.group())
    except FileNotFoundError as e:
        print("Fiel was not found:", e)
def DEmarcationLine():
    print("*************")
if __name__ == "__main__":
    main()
</code>
```

Here we search a file called "file.txt" that has words like "lenor" or "more" and that also matches some words that end with "ore". We have defined two functions to search that and we used "re" module.

Let us first see what is the content inside "file.txt". There are some misleading words and lines just to test our search.

<blockquote>
first line lenore
it is nine, second line and dine
third line and nevermore over
and fourth
fifth pine line lenore
and the tremor
here is more line
and a new line
i love you
where you are staying now?
i don't know
</blockquote>

After running our code we have found this search result.

<blockquote>
first line lenore
 third line and nevermore over
</blockquote>

```
fifth pine line lenore
************
lenore
nevermore
lenore
</blockquote>
```

It is a very simple regular expression example. It is beyond our scope to teach regular expression here but we can at least have some idea. I strongly recommend you move further. Search for "regular expression" on the Internet. You will find a lot of tutorials. Learning and understanding regular expression is very important. Whether you become a web developer, ethical hacker, or a Python programmer; regular expression will help.

CHAPTER 13

■ ■ ■

Exceptions, Catching Errors

I hope you have already written a lot of codes. If you had really done that, you would have encountered one or two errors. There are two distinguishable kinds of errors. The first is "SyntaxError". It means, you have error in your syntax. Consider this code:

```
<code>
>>> for i in range(10) print(i)
SyntaxError: invalid syntax
</code>
```

As you see, I forgot to use ":" in for loop. It is a syntax error.

Another error is "Exceptions". It means you write a code perfectly. There are no syntactical errors. But you forget to define a variable. Let us consider these lines of code:

```
<code>
>>> 10 * x
Traceback (most recent call last):
  File "<pyshell#1>", line 1, in <module>
    10 * x
NameError: name 'x' is not defined
>>> 10 / 0
Traceback (most recent call last):
  File "<pyshell#2>", line 1, in <module>
    10 / 0
ZeroDivisionError: division by zero
>>> '2' + 2
Traceback (most recent call last):
  File "<pyshell#3>", line 1, in <module>
    '2' + 2
TypeError: Can't convert 'int' object to str implicitly
>>> inputs = input("Please enter a number.")
Please enter a number.
>>> inputs + 2
Traceback (most recent call last):
  File "<pyshell#5>", line 1, in <module>
    inputs + 2
```

© Sanjib Sinha 2017
S. Sinha, *Beginning Ethical Hacking with Python*, DOI 10.1007/978-1-4842-2541-7_13

```
TypeError: Can't convert 'int' object to str implicitly
>>> inputs = input("Please enter a number.")
Please enter a number.12
>>> inputs - 10
Traceback (most recent call last):
  File "<pyshell#7>", line 1, in <module>
    inputs - 10
TypeError: unsupported operand type(s) for -: 'str' and 'int'
>>> int(inputs) - 10
2
>>>
</code>
```

As you see, there are lot of different kinds of errors. And in the last line we have come out from the error and gotten a perfect output. In the last error we get a "TypeError". We tried to subtract an integer from a string object. In the last step we converted that string input integer and the subtraction took place smoothly.

It is always good to catch those errors and get a nice output. The "try block" phrase has been used before. Now comes the time when we learn how we use those blocks to catch errors. Write down the code below in your text editor and save it as "CatchError.py".

```
<code>
#!/usr/bin/python3
def main():
    FileRead()
    DemarcationLine()
    LineStrip()
    DemarcationLine()
    CheckFileExtension()
def ReadFile(filename):
    files = open(filename)
    lines = files.readlines()
    for index, line in enumerate(lines):
        print(index, "=", line)
def StripFile(filename):
    files = open(filename)
    for lines in files:print(lines.strip())
def RaisingError(filename):
    if filename.endswith(".txt"):
        lines = open(filename)
        for line in lines:print(line.strip())
    else:
        raise ValueError("File must end with .txt")
def FileRead():
    try:
        ReadFile("../primary/files.txt") # path is okay, it reads file
    except IOError as e:
        print("Could not open file:", e)
```

```
def LineStrip():
    try:
        StripFile("primary/files.txt")
    except IOError as e:
        print("Could not open file:", e) # it will give error
def CheckFileExtension():
    try:
        RaisingError("../primary/file.rtf")
    except IOError as e:
        print("Could not open file:", e)
    except ValueError as e:
        print("Bad Filename:", e)
def DemarcationLine():
    print("*****************")
if __name__ == "__main__":
    main()
</code>
```

Run this file and you get this output:

<blockquote>
Could not open file: [Errno 2] No such file or directory: '../primary/files.txt'
****
Could not open file: [Errno 2] No such file or directory: 'primary/files.txt'
****
Bad Filename: File must end with .txt
</blockquote>

As an exercise, try to write this code with "Try" and "Except" and catch if there is any error.

```
<code>
#!/usr/bin/python3
def main():
    GetARangeOfNumber()
def GetARangeOfNumber():
    for index in IteratingStepByStep(1,123, 7):
        print(index, end=' ')
def IteratingStepByStep(start, stop, step):
    number = start
    while number <= stop:
        yield number
        number += step
if __name__ == "__main__":
    main()
</code>
```

## CHAPTER 14

Functions

Let us first define the function and try to know why function is being used in Python. Consider this code:

```
<code>
#!/usr/bin/python3
def main():
    print("This is main function.")
if __name__ == "__main__":
    main()
</code>
```

And the output is:

```
<blockquote>
This is main function.
</blockquote>
```

What does that mean? First of all, let us understand what function does mean. A function is used in any programming language to reuse code. Programmers are lazy and so they don't want to write again and again. And it is not a good idea to write the same thing again and again. So the concept of reusability comes in and we use function to do that.

You may consider a very simple example. Suppose we want to use a demarcation line again and again. Will you write like this again and again?

```
<code>
print("*************")
</code>
```

Or you will write a function and call it when it is necessary? Like this:

```
<code>
def DemarcationLine():
        print("*********")
```

© Sanjib Sinha 2017
S. Sinha, *Beginning Ethical Hacking with Python*, DOI 10.1007/978-1-4842-2541-7_14

```
DemarcationLine():
DemarcationLine():
DemarcationLine():
</code>
```

Each time you call the function "DemarcationLine()" it will print a demarcation line.

Now let us come to the first question. It is always a good practice to write functions inside main() function and you can call them any time. The flow control doesn't necessarily follow downward. You can test it:

```
<code>
def AnotherFunction():
    print("I am another function.")
def TestFunction():
    print("I am going to call another function.")
    AnotherFunction()
TestFunction()
<code>
```

It will print without any problem and give you this output:

```
<blockquote>
I am going to call another function.
I am anotheer function.
</blockquote>
```

Now we will write the above code differently.

```
<code>
def TestFunction():
    print("I am going to call another function.")
    AnotherFunction()

TestFunction()

def AnotherFunction():
    print("I am another function.")
</code>
```

A little bit of change in the position. We have not defined **AnotherFunction()** before **TestFunction()** and for that reason, it will give an error output:

```
<blockquote>
I am going to call another function.
Traceback (most recent call last):
  File "/home/hagudu/PycharmProjects/FirstPythonProject/functions/defining_
  functions.py", line 17, in <module>
```

```
    TestFunction()
  File "/home/hagudu/PycharmProjects/FirstPythonProject/functions/defining_
  functions.py", line 15, in TestFunction
    AnotherFunction()
NameError: name 'AnotherFunction' is not defined
</blockquote>
```

So each time you call a function inside another function, you need to define it first. But this problem can be solved if you define main() function first. Now consider this code:

```
<code>
#!/usr/bin/python3
def main():
    TestFunction()
def TestFunction():
    print("I am going to call another function.")
    AnotherFunction()
def AnotherFunction():
    print("I am another function.")
if __name__ == "__main__":
    main()
</code>
```

And here is the output:

```
<blockquote>
I am going to call another function.
I am another function.
</blockquote>
```

Now see, we did not bother about the position because all the functions are under main() function. Much more flexibility is now being added when you are using main() function like this. Another great advantage of using function is passing parameters or arguments through it.

```
<code>
#!/usr/bin/python3
def main():
    PassingParameters(1,2,3)
def PassingParameters(argument1, argument2, argument3):
    print("Here is our arguments:", argument1, argument2, argument3)
if __name__ == "__main__":
    main()
</code>
```

And the output is:

<blockquote>
Here is our arguments: 1 2 3
</blockquote>

We have passed three parameters or arguments and get the output as expected. But what happens if we forget to pass any argument? We don't want to get any nasty error message. We can manage that by two ways:

<code>
```
#!/usr/bin/python3
def main():
    PassingParameters(1)
def PassingParameters(argument1, argument2 = 4, argument3 = 6):
    print("Here is our arguments:", argument1, argument2, argument3)
if __name__ == "__main__":
    main()
```
</code>

And the output:

<blockquote>
Here is our arguments: 1 4 6
</blockquote>

It is called passing default values. We have passed two default values and when we actually call the function, it takes that default value. Now we can override these default values any time. Consider this one:

<code>
```
#!/usr/bin/python3
def main():
    PassingParameters(1, 10, 14)
def PassingParameters(argument1, argument2 = 4, argument3 = 6):
    print("Here is our arguments:", argument1, argument2, argument3)
if __name__ == "__main__":
    main()
```
</code>

And the output:

<blockquote>
Here is our arguments: 1 10 14
</blockquote>

We have overwritten the default values by passing new values and the output has changed accordingly. We can write this code this way also:

```
<code>
#!/usr/bin/python3
def main():
    PassingParameters(1)
def PassingParameters(argument1, argument2 = None, argument3 = 6):
    if argument2 == None:
        print("Here is our arguments:", argument1, argument2, argument3)
    else:
        print("Here is our arguments:", argument1, argument2, argument3)
if __name__ == "__main__":
    main()
</code>
```

And the output:

<blockquote>
Here is our arguments: 1 None 6
</blockquote>

What happens if we pass a new value for argument2? Consider this code:

```
<code>
#!/usr/bin/python3
def main():
    PassingParameters(1, 12)
def PassingParameters(argument1, argument2 = None, argument3 = 6):
    if argument2 == None:
        print("Here is our arguments:", argument1, argument2, argument3)
    else:
        print("Here is our arguments:", argument1, argument2, argument3)
if __name__ == "__main__":
    main()
</code>
```

And the output:

<blockquote>
Here is our arguments: 1 12 6
</blockquote>

In the next section we will see how lists of arguments work in a function.

Return Values

In Python a function can return any value. It can return any type of data: string, integer, object—anything. Let us return an object.

Consider this code:

```
<code>
#!/usr/bin/python3
def main():
    for index in ReturnValues():
        print(index, end=" ")
def ReturnValues():
    #return "Returning string."
    #return 56
    return range(10)
if __name__ == "__main__":
    main()
</code>
```

And the output:

<blockquote>
0 1 2 3 4 5 6 7 8 9
</blockquote>

We have returned range() object and got the value in our main() function.

Generate Functions

In Python we can generate functions. Let us explain it by step-by-step.

Consider this code first:

```
<code>
#!/usr/bin/python3
def main():
    RangeFunctions()
def RangeFunctions():
    for i in range(10):
        print(i, end=' ')
if __name__ == "__main__":
    main()
</code>
```

And the output is quite obvious:

<blockquote>
0 1 2 3 4 5 6 7 8 9
</blockquote>

You have probably found that the function RangeFunctions() has a limitation. It stops at 9, although the range is mentioned as 10. What can I do to include this number?

Let us write RangeFunctions() this way:

```
<code>
#!/usr/bin/python3
def main():
    for index in RangeFunctions(0, 10, 1):
        print(index, end=' ')

def RangeFunctions(start, stop, step):
    i = start
    while i <= stop:
        yield i
        i += step
if __name__ == "__main__":
    main()
</code>
```

And here is the output:

```
<blockquote>
0 1 2 3 4 5 6 7 8 9 10
</blockquote>
```

Here we have used the "yield" keyword. It is done because we have imagined that the code will progress step-by-step like we play a tape. After yielding one step it will stop and start from there and again start and go one step. You can just start from any point or stop at any point and progress by any step.

If we write like this:

```
for index in RangeFunctions(15, 1025, 102):
        print(index, end=' ')
```

The output will be:

```
15 117 219 321 423 525 627 729 831 933.
```

As you have seen, we can set the value of any argument as default. So we can write this function like this:

```
<code>
def AnotherRangeFunctions(start = 0, stop, step = 1):
    i = start
    while i <= stop:
        yield i
        i += step
</code>
```

And we may try to get the output by:

```
<code>
for index in AnotherRangeFunctions(25):
    print(index, end=' ')
</code>
```

But it gives us an error message:

File "/home/hagudu/PycharmProjects/FirstPythonProject/functions/generate-functions.py", line 18
    def AnotherRangeFunctions(start = 0, stop, step = 1):
SyntaxError: non-default argument follows default argument

Python does not support this. Can we solve this problem so that we can pass any number of arguments and control it without having any error message?

Consider this code:

```
<code>
def AnotherRangeFunctions(*args):
    numberOfArguments = len(args)

    if numberOfArguments < 1: raise TypeError('At least one argument is
    required.')
    elif numberOfArguments == 1:
        stop = args[0]
        start = 0
        step = 1
    elif numberOfArguments == 2:
        # start and stop will be tuple
        (start, stop) = args
        step = 1
    elif numberOfArguments == 3:
        # all start and stop and step will be tuple
        (start, stop, step) = args

    i = start
    while i <= stop:
        yield i
        i += step
</code>
```

Write down every line and take notes side-by-side. Add comments where you feel that an explanation is necessary.

Lists of Arguments

In Python sometimes you need arbitrary number of arguments and you have to name them. Let us write this code:

```
<code>
#!/usr/bin/python3
def main():
    PassingListsOfArguments(1, 2, 3, 5, 7, 45, 98, 56, 4356, 90876543)
    PassingAnotherListsOfArguments(1, 2, 3, 5, 7, 45, 98, 76, 987654, 3245,
    2345, 98760)

def PassingListsOfArguments(arg1, arg2, arg3, arg4, *args):
    print(arg1, arg2, arg3, arg4, args)

def PassingAnotherListsOfArguments(param1, param2, *params):
    print(param1, param2)
    for index in params:
        if index == 76:
            x = 10
            y = index + x
            print("We are going to add 10 with", index, "and the new value
            is:", y)
            continue
        print(index, end=' ')

if __name__ == "__main__":
    main()
</code>
```

And the output goes like this:

<blockquote>
1 2 3 5 (7, 45, 98, 56, 4356, 90876543)
1 2 3 5 7 45 98 We are going to add 10 with 76 and the new value is: 86
987654 3245 2345 98760
</blockquote>

In our code, ***args** or ***params** mean lists of arguments. You can pass any number of arguments through them. In code

```
def PassingListsOfArguments(arg1, arg2, arg3, arg4, *args):
```

means you need to pass four arguments first. That is compulsory. After that, the number of arguments may vary. But the arbitrary number of arguments comes out as "tuple". See the output of this function:

1 2 3 5 (7, 45, 98, 56, 4356, 90876543)

The latter part is obviously a tuple and you can iterate through it.

Named Arguments

Sometimes it is important to use named arguments in Python. And we get those named arguments in a dictionary format.

Consider this code:

```
<code>
#!/usr/bin/python3
def main():
    NamedArguments(name = 'Sanjib', address = 'Pluto', hobby = "Gardening")
def NamedArguments(**kwargs):
    for key in kwargs:
        print(key, "=", kwargs[key])
if __name__ == "__main__":
    main()
</code>
```

And the output:

```
<blockquote>
hobby = Gardening
name = Sanjib
address = Pluto
</blockquote>
```

As it is a dictionary output, it is not ordered. You can sort it alphabetically.

Let us consider a fairly long code where we can use every kind of passing argument.

```
<code>
#!/usr/bin/python3
def main():
    NamedArguments(name = 'Sanjib', address = 'Pluto', hobby = "Gardening")
    DemarcationLine()
    AnotherNamedArguments('Hi', 1235, 1,2,3, one = 1, two = 2, three = 3)

def NamedArguments(**kwargs):
    for key in kwargs:
        print(key, "=", kwargs[key])
```

```
def AnotherNamedArguments(arg1, arg2, *args, **kwargs):
    print(arg1, arg2)
    for index in args:
        print(index, end=' ')
    DemarcationLine()
    for keys in kwargs:
        print(keys, "=", kwargs[keys])

def DemarcationLine():
    print("********")

if __name__ == "__main__":
    main()
</code>
```

Here is the output:

```
<blockquote>
hobby = Gardening
address = Pluto
name = Sanjib
********
Hi 1235
1 2 3 ********
three = 3
two = 2
one = 1
</blockquote>
```

CHAPTER 15

Classes

If you are a complete beginner, you are probably hearing for the first time about "object-oriented programming and class." Let us give a brief introduction to object-oriented programming (OOP).

Object-Oriented Methodology

It is based on real world programming. An object is a representation of a real world entity. If there is an object, there must be a class or blueprint behind it. In that class, the behavior of that object is designed or described in detail. These details consist of all the properties and actions that the object performs. There could be many types of objects coming from different classes and they might have relationships. It could be very complicated, but you can always break those objects from one another and make some changes. The advantage of object orientation is that when you work on a part of a big, complicated project, the other part remains unaffected. Our goal is simple. We want to join different objects to create big, complicated software. At the same time, we want to make the relations of those objects as loose as possible.

A car object is built of many other objects like tire, wheel, engine, accelerator, etcetera. If you get a flat tire does the engine stop? They are interrelated and depend on one another. But finally you can work on them individually without affecting the other. That is object orientation.

Consider an object, "GoodHuman". This object must be different from another object, "BadHuman". Both come from the "Human" class. Now these two objects might have interrelationships and data interactions. Can you imagine how many kinds of properties and methods there are in the "Human" class? It could be very complex. Imagine a situation where a "BadHuman" does something ugly. At the same time, a "GoodHuman" does something good. Whoever does whatever thing, life goes on and that is also object orientation.

The Foundation of Object Orientation

Object orientation is a type of methodology used for building software applications. An object-oriented program consists of classes, objects and methods. The object-oriented methodology in software development revolves around a single concept called the object.

© Sanjib Sinha 2017
S. Sinha, *Beginning Ethical Hacking with Python*, DOI 10.1007/978-1-4842-2541-7_15

You can develop software by breaking the application into component objects. These objects interact with each other when the whole application is put together. An object is a combination of messages and data. The object receives and sends messages and those messages contain data or information.

You (an object) interact with your television (another object) via messages sent through a remote controller (another object).

Consider another real world example of a football. A football has a boundary. It has a specific defined property like bouncing. You can direct or apply few specific actions by kicking it or throwing it.

An object has a state. It may display behavior. It has a unique ID.

The difference between an object and class is subtle but important. Whereas a class is an abstract concept, an object is a concrete entity. From a class, objects with specific properties can be created or instantiated. That is why an object is often called an instance of a class.

One of the major features of object-oriented programming is "polymorphism." Polymorphism is the capability of something to assume different forms. In object-oriented programming, polymorphism is the property that a message can mean different things depending on the objects receiving it. The message "Accelerate" means one thing if it sent to an object "OldCar". But it means a different thing if it is sent to the object "NewCar". It is a natural concept that can be applied to objects. It also means that similar objects often accept the same message but do different things.

Consider a web page. It is an object. There are billions of such objects around us. When you send a request to an object like a web page, you actually apply a verb "GET" to a noun "WebPage". Now every "WebPage" object does not behave the same way when the "GET" verb is applied. Someone opens up a PDF file, someone simply shows some texts and pictures and someone may harm your computer. When you double-click a file, it may execute if it is an executable file. Or it may open up in a text editor if it is a text file. The message is same. That is "Double-Click". But the behavior displayed by the file object depends on the object itself.

This is polymorphism. You will learn it by heart as you progress through this chapter.

The advantage of Python classes is that they provide all the standard features of object-oriented programming. It has the class inheritance mechanism. That allows multiple base classes. A derived class can override any methods of its base class or classes, and a method can call the method of a base class with the same name. Objects can contain arbitrary amounts and kinds of data.

Finally, remember, in Python everything is an object. It means there is an abstraction or encapsulation behind it. You need to understand the abstraction first and then you create your own abstraction.

Understanding Classes and Objects

You cannot understand theory unless you implement that concept into the real world. Let us see what we have learned.

1. **Classes are when you create your own object.**

2. **A class is a blueprint for an object.**

3. **An object is an instance of a class.**

Let us see how we can build a class and later create a few instances from it. Consider this code:

```
<code>
#!/usr/bin/python3
class Robot:
    def __init__(self):
        pass
    def WalkLikeARobot(self):
        print("walks like a robot.")
    def CareLikeARobot(self):
        print("takes care like a robot.")
robu1 = Robot()
print(type(robu1))
print(id(robu1))
robu2 = Robot()
print(type(robu2))
print(id(robu2))
del robu2
def main():
    robu = Robot()
    print(type(robu))
    print(id(robu))
if __name__ == "__main__":
    main()
</code>
```

In this code, we have class definition of "Robot". Here "class" is the key word. Next to it is a ":" sign, which means a class definition will follow a suite or block of codes. After we have defined the class "Robot", we have three methods.

And they are :

```
def __init__(self):
        pass
    def WalkLikeARobot(self):
        print("walks like a robot.")
    def CareLikeARobot(self):
        print("takes care like a robot.")
```

The first one is the special method. When a class is instantiated, this method will be called first. "__init__" means initialization. The class is initialized. Two other methods follow it. Those methods are self-explanatory. Methods are action verbs. When we create a robot object and we call those methods, we actually tell them to do something. In our class we defined what they will do.

In this code we created three robot objects. And finally we did not tell them to do anything. We have just seen how they are different from one another. We have tested their type and ID. Look, each object has a different ID. So this is a major point. Each object or instance created from a class, has its own individuality.

Now see the output:

```
<blockquote>
<class '__main__.Robot'>
140445354614624
<class '__main__.Robot'>
140445354668160
<class '__main__.Robot'>
140445354668160
</blockquote>
```

The next lines of code are a little bit longer but I strongly suggest that you write them on your own text editor and run the program to see that you get the same output.

```
<code>
#!/usr/bin/python3
class Robots:
    def __init__(self):
        pass
    def WalkLikeARobot(self, style):
        self.style = style
        return self.style
    def CareLikeARobot(self):
        print("takes care like a robot.")
class Humans:
    def __init__(self, nature = "good"):
        self.nature = nature
    def GoodHumanBeing(self):
        print("need not repeat, a good human being is always", self.nature)
    def BadHUmanBeing(self):
        self.nature = "need not repeat, bad human being is always bad."
        print(self.nature)
    def WalkLikeARobot(self, style):
        self.style = style
        return self.style
def main():
    robu = Robots()
    robu.CareLikeARobot()
    print(robu.WalkLikeARobot("walks like a robot"))
    GoodMan = Humans()
    print(GoodMan.nature)
    GoodMan.GoodHumanBeing()
    BadMan = Humans()
    BadMan.nature = "bad"
    print(BadMan.nature)
    BadMan.BadHUmanBeing()
```

```
    print(BadMan.WalkLikeARobot("he is human but walks like a robot"))
if __name__ == "__main__":
    main()
</code>
```

In the above snippet of code, we have two classes. One is "Robot", that we wrote earlier. The other class is "Human". In the "Human" class, we have defined this special method like this:

```
def __init__(self, nature = "good"):
    self.nature = nature
```

What does this mean? It means when we create a human instance of this class, we assume that the nature of human object will by default be good. Unfortunately, it does not happen in the real world. Keeping that in mind, we also write this line: "self.nature = nature". It means self nature or the nature of the instance will be good if we do not explicitly mention that it is "Bad" or something else.

In the following steps, when we create a bad human instance, we explicitly change the nature. Remember, each method is the action part of that object. An object is a noun and it does something. In any software application it follows the same rule. An example of polymorphism is also there. In both classes, "Robot" and "Human", we have defined a method:

```
def WalkLikeARobot(self, style):
    self.style = style
    return self.style
```

When we apply this same verb to the different Robot and Human objects, it displays different behavior. If you run this code, it gives us an output like this:

```
<blockquote>
takes care like a robot.
walks like a robot
good
need not repeat, a good human being is always good
bad
need not repeat, bad human being is always bad.
he is human but walks like a robot
</blockquote>
```

When a Robot instance walks like a robot, it displays: **walks like a robot;** but when an instance of Human walks like a robot, it displays: **he is human but walks like a robot.** This is nothing but a simple example of polymorphism. When the same verb applies to two different objects, depending on the nature of the object it gives a different output.

Actually, we change this behavior by passing two different arguments. Suppose, instead of a single argument, we pass a dictionary of values. See how the power is magnified. Consider a simple code below:

```
<code>
print(type(BadMan.WalkLikeARobot(dict(one=1, two=2))))
st = BadMan.WalkLikeARobot(dict(one=1, two=2))
for keys in sorted(st):
    print(keys, st[keys])
ws = BadMan.WalkLikeARobot({'one':56, 'two':2})
for keys in sorted(ws):
    print(keys, ws[keys])
</code>
```

Here is the output:

```
<blockquote>
<class 'dict'>
one 1
two 2
one 56
two 2
</blockquote>
```

You can add more key, value pairs to this dictionary and run this code to see what happens.

Write Your Own Game, "Good Vs Bad"

So far we have learned many things. I hope you have written the codes and tested them and it executed perfectly. Now the time has come to write a simple game in Python. It is a game called "Good Vs Bad." The game is simple. But as a beginner you may find this code a bit longer. Write it down. Try to add more features.

If you are in a Linux environment, save this file as "good-vs-bad.py" and change the file executable by running this command:

```
Sudo chmod +x  good-vs-bad.py
```

And then run it on your terminal like this:

```
./ good-vs-bad.py
```

If you are in Windows, run the IDLE and save the file as "good-vs-bad.py". Press F5 and play the game.

It looks like this on the computer screen:

Figure 15-1. *Playing Python game on Windows IDE*

In the background, the code shows and you may play the game on Python Shell. The code is like this:

```
<code>
#!/usr/bin/python3
class Robots:
    def __init__(self):
        pass
    def WalkLikeARobot(self, WalkingStyle):
        self.WalkingStyle = WalkingStyle
        return self.WalkingStyle
    def CareLikeARobot(self):
        print("takes care like a robot.")
class Humans:
    def __init__(self, nature = "good"):
        self.nature = nature
    def GoodHumanBeing(self):
        print("need not repeat, a good human being is always", self.nature)
    def BadHUmanBeing(self):
        self.nature = "need not repeat, bad human being is always bad."
        print(self.nature)
```

```
    def WalkLikeARobot(self, WalkingStyle):
        self.WalkingStyle = WalkingStyle
        return self.WalkingStyle
def main():
    robu = Robots()
    # robu.CareLikeARobot()
    # print(robu.WalkLikeARobot("A robot walks like a robot and nothing
    happens."))
    GoodMan = Humans()
    # print(GoodMan.nature)
    # GoodMan.GoodHumanBeing()
    BadMan = Humans()
    # BadMan.nature = "bad"
    # print(BadMan.nature)
    # BadMan.BadHUmanBeing()
    # print(BadMan.WalkLikeARobot("he is human but walks like a robot"))
    # when a bad man wlaks like a robot many things happen
    WhenABadManWalksLikeARobot = BadMan.WalkLikeARobot(dict(change = 'he
    becomes a monster inside',
                                act = 'he kills fellow people',
                                feel = 'he enjoys torturing animals',
                                care = 'he cares for none',
                                look = 'he looks a normal human being',
                                state = 'finally he destroys himself'))
    # there are lot of actions that take place
    print("What happens when a Bad Man walks like a Robot?")
    change = input("Tell us what kind of change may take place inside him?\n
    Choose between 'monster' and 'angel',"
                "and type here...>>>>")
    WhenABadManWalksLikeARobot['change'] = change
    reward = 0
    if change == 'monster':
        print("You have won the first round:", change)
        reward = 1000
        print("You have won ", reward, "points.")
        print("What does he do? :", WhenABadManWalksLikeARobot['act'])
        change = input("Now tell us what the monster feels inside while
        killing people?\n Choose between 'great' and 'sad',"
                    "and type here...>>>>")
        WhenABadManWalksLikeARobot['change'] = change
        if change == 'great':
            print("You have won the second round:")
            reward = 10000
            print("You have won ", reward, "points.")
            print("What he feels inside? :", WhenABadManWalksLikeARobot
            ['feel'])
            change = input("Tell us does the monster care for anyone?\n
            Choose between 'yes' and 'no',"
```

```
                "and type here...>>>>")
        WhenABadManWalksLikeARobot['change'] = change
        if change == 'no':
            print("You have won the third round:")
            reward = 100000
            print("You have won ", reward, "points.")
            print("What he feels inside? :", WhenABadManWalksLikeARobot
            ['care'])
            change = input("Tell us does the monster look like a normal
            human being?\n Choose between 'yes' and 'no',"
                "and type here...>>>>")
            WhenABadManWalksLikeARobot['change'] = change
            if change == 'yes':
                print("You have won the fourth round:")
                reward = 1000000
                print("You have won ", reward, "points.")
                print("What does he look like? :", WhenABadManWalksLike
                ARobot['look'])
                change = input("Tell us what happens to the monster
                finally? Does he destroy himself\n Choose between 'yes'
                and 'no',"
                            "and type here...>>>>")
                WhenABadManWalksLikeARobot['change'] = change
                if change == 'yes':
                    print("You have won the fifth round:")
                    reward = 100000000
                    print("You have won Jackpot.", reward, "points.")
                else:
                    print("You have changed the course of game. It ends
                    here. You have lost", reward - 100000, "points.")
            else:
                print("You have changed the course of game. It ends
                here. You have lost", reward - 1000, "points.")
        else:
            print("You have changed the course of game. It ends here.
            You have lost", reward - 100, "points.")
    else:
        print("You have changed the course of game. It ends here. You
        have lost", reward - 10, "points.")
else:
    print("You have changed the course of game. It ends here and you
    have won no point.")
if __name__ == "__main__":
    main()
</code>
```

And the output on your Python Shell looks like this:

```
<blockquote>
What happens when a Bad Man walks like a Robot?
Tell us what kind of change may take place inside him?
  Choose between 'monster' and 'angel',and type here...>>>>monster
You have won the first round: monster
You have won  1000 points.
What does he do? : he kills fellow people
Now tell us what the monster feels inside while killing people?
  Choose between 'great' and 'sad',and type here...>>>>great
You have won the second round:
You have won  10000 points.
What he feels inside? : he enjoys torturing animals
Tell us does the monster care for anyone?
  Choose between 'yes' and 'no',and type here...>>>>no
You have won the third round:
You have won  100000 points.
What he feels inside? : he cares for none
Tell us does the monster look like a normal human being?
  Choose between 'yes' and 'no',and type here...>>>>yes
You have won the fourth round:
You have won  1000000 points.
What does he look like? : he looks a normal human being
Tell us what happens to the monster finally? Does he destroy himself
  Choose between 'yes' and 'no',and type here...>>>>yes
You have won the fifth round:
You have won Jackpot. 100000000 points.
</blockquote>
```

Since I wrote the code, I won the game. But there are a few tricks. In those tricky parts, if you failed and supplied wrong inputs you would lose.

Primary Class and Object

Now primary class and object should no longer be difficult. You can write a Human class and pass one default argument like "kind" in the initialization process. You can set it as "good". Now if you want to create a good human being you need not pass any extra argument. In the next step, when you apply a verb like "BeingHuman()" to the good human being, it is by default good. If you want to create a bad human being, you can change that default argument and make it bad.

```
<code>
#!/usr/bin/python3
class Human:
    def __init__(self, kind = "good"):
        self.kind = kind
```

```
        def BeingHuman(self):
            return self.kind
def main():
    good = Human()
    bad = Human("bad")
    print(good.BeingHuman ())
    print(bad.BeingHuman ())
if __name__ == "__main__":
    main()
</code>
```

The output is quite obvious:

```
<blockquote>
good
bad
</blockquote>
```

There are a few things you need to understand. Why do we use "self"? What does that mean? Consider the code below.

```
<code>
#!/usr/bin/python3
class MySelf:
    def __init__(self, name, quantity):
        self.name = name
        self.quantity = quantity
    def Eat(self):
        print(self.name, "eats", self.quantity, "bananas each day.")
def main():
    hagu = MySelf("Hagu", 2)
    mutu = MySelf("Mutu", 3)
    hagu.Eat()
    mutu.Eat()
if __name__ == "__main__":
    main()
</code>
```

In this code of class "MySelf" we have two methods. One is the special constructor method "__init__" and the other is "Eat()". You notice that each method has a special argument: "self". Actually, it references the object that is going to be created. When we write a class, we assume that instances will be created. In this case, we created two objects, "hagu" and "mutu". When we apply the verb "Eat()" or call the method to the objects, it is as though they pass through the method. We set the names and the numbers of bananas they eat. And the output of this code is like this:

<blockquote>
Hagu eats 2 bananas each day.
Mutu eats 3 bananas each day.
</blockquote>

But we need more concrete examples. We want to connect to our databases from our applications. To do that we need a class where we will have methods and properties that will connect to databases.

Suppose we have two different set-ups. We have a MySQL database and, in addition, we want to create an SQLite connection. To do that we can write two separate classes and set the connection in the constructor part or initialization method. So that when we create an instance, the connection to the database is set up automatically.

Consider the code:

```python
#!/usr/bin/python3
import sqlite3
import mysql.connector
from mysql.connector import Error
class MySQLiteConnection:
    def __init__(self):
        db = sqlite3.connect('testdb.db')
        db.commit()
        print("Connected to SqLite3")
class MyMySQLConnection:
    def __init__(self):
        try:
        ### you can either use a dictionary object or you can connect
        directly ###
        ### using a dictioanry object ###
            kwargs = dict(host = 'localhost', database = 'python_mysql',
            user = 'root', password = 'pass')
            conn = mysql.connector.connect(**kwargs)
        ### connecting directly ###
            connection = mysql.connector.connect(host = 'localhost',
                                                  database = 'python_mysql',
                                                  user = 'root',
                                                  password = 'pass')
            if connection.is_connected():
                print("Connected to MySQL from 'conneection' object")
            # if conn.is_connected():
            #     print("Connected from 'conn' object")
        except Error as e:
            print(e)
        finally:
            connection.close()
def main():
    ConnectToMySQL = MyMySQLConnection()
```

```
    ConenctToSqlite = MySQLiteConnection()
if __name__ == "__main__":
    main()
</code>
```

We create two instances or objects of **MyMySQLConnection()** and **MySQLiteConnection()** classes and put them into two separate variables. Connections are being set up and in the output section we see this:

```
<blockquote>
Connected to MySQL from 'connection' object
Connected to SqLite3
</blockquote>
```

But this is an extremely simple example and written badly. We should develop this code so that each instance of MySQLConnection and SQLiteConnection classes can not only connect to the database but also retrieve data from a table.

Let us replace our old code with this:

```
<code>
#!/usr/bin/python3

import sqlite3
import mysql.connector
from mysql.connector import MySQLConnection, Error

class MySQLiteConnection:
    def __init__(self, db = sqlite3.connect('test.db')):
        self.db = db
        db.row_factory = sqlite3.Row
        print("Connected to SqLite3")
    def Retrieve(self):
        print("Retreiving values from table test1 of SqLite database test")
        read = self.db.execute('select * from test1 order by i1')
        for row in read:
            print(row['t1'])
class MyMySQLConnection:
    def __init__(self, kwargs = dict(host = 'localhost', database =
    'testdb', user = 'root', password = 'pass')):
        try:
        ### you can either use a dictionary object or you can connect
        directly ###
        ### using a dictioanry object ###
            self.kwargs = kwargs
            conn = mysql.connector.connect(**kwargs)
```

```
            if conn.is_connected():
                print("Connected to MySql database testdb from 'conn'
                object")
        except Error as e:
            print(e)
        finally:
            conn.close()
    def Retrieve(self):
        print("Retreiving records from MySql database testdb.")
        try:
            conn = MySQLConnection(**self.kwargs)
            cursor = conn.cursor()
            cursor.execute("SELECT * FROM EMPLOYEE")
            rows = cursor.fetchall()
            print('Total Row(s):', cursor.rowcount)
            for row in rows:
                print("First Name = ", row[0])
                print("Second Name = ", row[1])
                print("Age = ", row[2])
                print("Sex = ", row[3])
                print("Salary = ", row[4])
        except Error as e:
            print(e)
        finally:
            cursor.close()
            conn.close()
def main():
    ConnectToMySQL = MyMySQLConnection()
    ConnectToMySQL.Retrieve()
    ConenctToSqLite = MySQLiteConnection()
    ConenctToSqLite.Retrieve()
if __name__ == "__main__":
    main()
</code>
```

We have connected to each database with the initialization process and then apply one verb, "Retrieve()", to each object. We have also imported many database modules that you have not learned yet.

You will learn them in due process. But our purpose is served. We create two separate database objects. One is a MySQL connection object and another is an SQLite connection object. After that, with those objects we are able to retrieve separate data from two different tables.

First look at the output:

```
<blockquote>
Connected to MySql database testdb from 'conn' object
Retreiving records from MySql database testdb.
Total Row(s): 3
```

```
First Name =  Mac
Second Name =  Mohan
Age =  20
Sex =  M
Salary =  2000.0
First Name =  Mac
Second Name =  Mohan
Age =  20
Sex =  M
Salary =  2000.0
First Name =  Mac
Second Name =  Mohan
Age =  20
Sex =  M
Salary =  2000.0
Connected to SqLite3
Retreiving values from table test1 of SqLite database test
Babu
Mana
Bappa
Babua
Anju
Patai
GasaBuddhu
Tapas
</blockquote>
```

The output says, the MySQL database "testdb" has a table called "Employee" and there are several rows like name, sex, salary, etc. Second, we have an SQLite3 database "test1" which has a table called "test1" which has many rows that contain few names.

Accessing Object Data

When an object is created from a class it is quite obvious that it will have some kind of data. The question is how we can access that data? What is the proper way? We must access that data in a way so that we can keep a track of that. Consider this code below:

```
<code>
#!/usr/bin/python3
class Human:
    def __init__(self, height = 5.08):
        self.height = height
def main():
    ramu = Human()
    print(ramu.height)
    ramu.height = 5.11 # it is called side effect and hard to track
```

```
     print(ramu.height)
if __name__ == "__main__":
    main()
</code>
```

In this code we see Human class with a default height, which is 5.08. When we create an object, this height is set automatically unless we change it or mention it explicitly. We can also set any property outside that object. In the next line we have written **ramu. height = 5.11.**

We can set any object property like this. But this is called side effect and it is very hard to track. So we need to do that in a more structured manner. How we can do that? Let us see the output of this code first.

```
<blockquote>
5.08
5.11
</blockquote>
```

You see the height changes and we don't know what is the proper height of object "ramu". To solve this problem, the accessor method is implemented. The accessor methods are methods that first set the value and then through that method you can get the value.

```
<code>
#!/usr/bin/python3
class Human:
    def __init__(self):
        pass
    # accessor
    def set_height(self, height):
        self.height = height
    def get_height(self):
        return self.height
def main():
    ramu = Human()
    # ramu.height = 5.11 # it is called side effect and hard to track
    ramu.set_height(5.12)
    print(ramu.get_height())
if __name__ == "__main__":
    main()
</code>
<blockquote>
5.12
</blockquote>
```

But we're still missing something. We want to add more flexibilities so that with less code we can get more jobs done.

```
<code>
#!/usr/bin/python3
class Human:
    def __init__(self, **kwargs):
        self.variables = kwargs
    def set_manyVariables(self, **kwargs):
        self.variables = kwargs
    def set_variables(self, key, value):
        self.variables[key] = value
    def get_variables(self, key):
        return self.variables.get(key, None)
def main():
    mana = Human(name = 'Mana')
    print("Object Mana's name:", mana.variables['name'])
    ManaName = mana.variables['name']
    mana.set_variables('class', 'two')
    print(ManaName, "reads at class", mana.get_variables('class'))
    mana.set_manyVariables(school = 'balika school', height = 4.54)
    print(ManaName, "has height of", mana.variables['height'], "and her
    school's name is", mana.variables['school'])
    babu = Human(name = 'Babu', student_of = 'Class Three', reads_at = '
    Balak School', height = 5.21)
    BabuName = babu.variables['name']
    print(BabuName, "he is a student of", babu.variables['student_of'], "and
    he reads at",
        babu.variables['reads_at'], "and his height is", babu.
        variables['height'])
if __name__ == "__main__":
    main()
</code>
```

In this code snippet we have many options open to us. We have set our variables in a dictionary format. After that we can get the value through the key.

```
<blockquote>
Object Mana's name: Mana
Mana reads at class two
Mana has height of 4.54 and her school's name is balika school
Babu he is a student of Class Three and he reads at Balak School and his
height is 5.21
</blockquote>
```

This is not the only method to tackle object data. As you progress you will see a lot of different examples of handling data.

Polymorphism

Polymorphism is a very important concept in object-oriented programming. The basic thing is when we apply the same verb on two different objects, depending on the objects, they react differently. When we put up an old house for sale it fetches a certain value. But when we put up a new house for sale it fetches a higher price and value. So in this case when we apply "sale" method or "sale" verb to different objects, they behave differently.

<code>
```
#!/usrbin/python3
class Table:
    def __init__(self):
        pass
    def ItHolds(self):
        print("A table holds books, writing pads on it.")
    def YouCanWriteOnit(self):
        print("You can write on a table.")

class Book:
    def __init__(self):
        pass
    def ItHelps(self):
        print("A book helps us to know something new.")

def main():
    MyTable = Table()
    MyBook = Book()
    MyTable.ItHolds()
    MyTable.YouCanWriteOnit()
    MyBook.ItHelps()
if __name__ == "__main__":
    main()
```
</code>

These are quite simple classes and the output is also very simple.

<blockquote>
```
A table holds things on it.
You can write on a table.
A book helps us to know something new.
```
</blockquote>

This output may change drastically when you apply the same verbs or methods to the objects of "Table" and "Book" classes. Consider the following codes.

<code>
```
#!/usrbin/python3
```
</code>

```
class Table:
    def __init__(self):
        pass

    def Get(self):
        print("Please get me that table.")
    def Put(self):
        print("Please put the table on the corner of the room.")
    def Destroy(self):
        print("Some people came and they did not want us to read and write.
        They destroted the table.")
class Book:
    def __init__(self):
        pass
     def Get(self):
        print("Please get me that book.")
    def Put(self):
        print("We put some new books on the table.")
    def Destroy(self):
        print("Some people came and they did not want us to read and write.
        They destroyed the book.")
def main():
    MyTable = Table()
    MyBook = Book()
    InMistake(MyBook)
    Intentionally(MyTable)
def InMistake(Table):
    Table.Get()
    Table.Put()
    Table.Destroy()
def Intentionally(Book):
    Book.Get()
    Book.Put()
    Book.Destroy()
if __name__ == "__main__":
    main()
<code>
```

There are three methods: Get, Put, and Destroy. You see how the table and book objects react differently to those methods.

```
<blockquote>
Please get me that book.
We put some new books on the table.
Some people came and they did not want us to read and write. They destroyed
the book.
Please get me that table.
```

115

Please put the table on the corner of the room.
Some people came and they did not want us to read and write. They destroyed
the table.
</blockquote>

Using Generators

In Python, a generator object is used in a context where iteration is necessary. Normally, in this case, we rely on two methods: **def __init__(self, *args)** and **def __iter__(self).** We set the logic in the constructor method and iterate through it by the **def __iter__(self)** function.

<code>
```
#!/usr/bin/python3
class InclusiveRange:
    def __init__(self, *args):
        numberOfArguments = len(args)
        if numberOfArguments < 1: raise TypeError('At least one argument is
        required.')
        elif numberOfArguments == 1:
            self.stop = args[0]
            self.start = 0
            self.step = 1
        elif numberOfArguments == 2:
            # start and stop will be tuple
            (self.start, stop) = args
            self.step = 1
        elif numberOfArguments == 3:
            # all start and stop and step will be tuple
            (self.start, self.stop, self.step) = args
        else: raise TypeError("Maximum three arguments. You gave {}".
        format(numberOfArguments))

    def __iter__(self):
        i = self.start
        while i <= self.stop:
            yield i
            i += self.step

def main():
    ranges = InclusiveRange(5, 210, 10)
    for x in ranges:
        print(x, end=' ')
if __name__ == "__main__":
    main()
```
</code>

This code means you can control the range of iteration. We start from 5 and then end at 210. In each step we progress by 10.

<blockquote>
5 15 25 35 45 55 65 75 85 95 105 115 125 135 145 155 165 175 185 195 205
</blockquote>

We can get the same effect without using those methods. We can simply write this way.

<code>

```
## the function below is perfectly working also but that is not a generator
##

def RangeFunctions(self, *args):
    numberOfArguments = len(args)
    if numberOfArguments < 1: raise TypeError('At least one argument is
    required.')
    elif numberOfArguments == 1:
        self.stop = args[0]
        self.start = 0
        self.step = 1
    elif numberOfArguments == 2:
        # start and stop will be tuple
        (self.start, stop) = args
        self.step = 1
    elif numberOfArguments == 3:
        # all start and stop and step will be tuple
        (self.start, self.stop, self.step) = args
    else: raise TypeError("Maximum three arguments. You gave {}".
    format(numberOfArguments))

    i = self.start
    while i <= self.stop:
        yield i
        i += self.step
```

</code>

Inheritance

Inheritance is an equally important concept in object-oriented programming. There is a parent class and a child class. The child class usually inherits all the properties and methods from the parent class. At the same time, it can change all the properties and methods according to the situation.

The way a child class inherits is very simple. When we declare a child class we write the name of the parent class inside the child class like this: ChildClass(ParentClass).

```
<code>
#!/usr/bin/python3
class AllUsers:
    def __init__(self):
        pass
    def Register(self):
        print("Please Register")
    def Login(self):
        print("Welcome Member.")
class Admin(AllUsers):
    def __init__(self):
        pass
    def Register(self):
        print("Admins need not register")
    def Login(self):
        print("Welcome Admin")
class Members(AllUsers):
    def __init__(self):
        pass
def main():
    admin = Admin()
    admin.Register()
    admin.Login()
    member = Members()
    member.Register()
    member.Login()
if __name__ == "__main__":
    main()
</code>
```

The Parent class is "**AllUsers()**". There are two child classes: "**Admin**" and "**Members**". Through the child classes we inherit all the properties and methods from the parent class. In the parent class, we mentioned that all users should register and log in. Now in the child class "**Admin**" we override the methods, but in the "**Members**" class we do not change them. When we create an instance of "**Admin**" class, it has its own properties and methods. But in "**Members**" class, we decided not to override the parent class methods. It is evident in the following output.

```
<blockquote>
Admins need not register
Welcome Admin
Please Register
Welcome Member.
</blockquote>
```

Decorator

Decorators are special functions that return functions. Normally, to set a property of object we usually get it through another function.

```
<code>
#!/usr/bin/python3
class Dog:

    def __init__(self, **kwargs):
        self.properties = kwargs
    def get_properties(self):
        return self.properties
    def set_properties(self, key):
        self.properties.get(key, None)

def main():
    lucky = Dog(nature = 'obedient')
    print(lucky.properties.get('nature'))

if __name__ == "__main__":
    main()
</code>
```

The output is quite simple.

<blockquote>
obedient
</blockquote>

In Python, "Decorator" is simply a method by which we decorate an accessor method for a variable, and the function starts behaving like a property. The beauty of this decorator is, you can use the function as a property and after creating the object you can control the property—setting and getting it. See the following code.

```
<code>
#!/usr/bin/python3
class Dog:

    def __init__(self, **kwargs):
        self.properties = kwargs
    @property
    def Color(self):
        return self.properties.get('color', None)
    @Color.setter
    def Color(self, color):
        self.properties['color'] = color
```

```
    @Color.deleter
    def Color(self):
        del self.properties['color']
def main():
    lucky = Dog()
# now we are going to use the decorator function as a normal property
    lucky.Color = 'black and yellow'
    print(lucky.Color)

if __name__ == "__main__":
    main()
</code>
```

The output is as expected:

```
<blockquote>
black and yellow
</blockquote>
```

It is a very simple example where we see that a usual syntax of function can be written as a property syntax. It is more convenient when we use this decorator method in saving files inside a database.

In the last chapter, we will see the web application "Flask." We will see how we can use this decorator to route our web pages.

CHAPTER 16

String Methods

In Python a string is an object. As an instance of "class string" it can call any function or property. We can change a string into upper case by simply calling a function upper().
Let us open our terminal and type this:

```
<code>
hagudu@hagudu-H81M-S1:~$ python3

Python 3.4.0 (default, Jun 19 2015, 14:20:21)

[GCC 4.8.2] on linux

Type "help", "copyright", "credits" or "license" for more information.

>>> 'this is a string'

'this is a string'

>>> s = 'this is a string'

>>> s

'this is a string'

>>> s.upper()

'THIS IS A STRING'

>>> s = 'this is a string now we are going to add an integer into it as
string {}'

>>> s.format(100)

'this is a string now we are going to add an integer into it as string 100'

>>> 'in python2 it was written like %d' % 100
```

```
'in python2 it was written like 100'

>>>
```
</code>

We have just changed a string to upper case and also added an integer into that string.

In Python 2 it was done like this:

```
'in python2 it was written like %d' % 100
```

But in Python 3.4 and onwards we will not use it anymore. We will use format() function like this:

>>> s = 'this is a string now we are going to add an integer into it as string {}'
>>> s.format(100)
'this is a string now we are going to add an integer into it as string 100'

<code>
```
>>> s = 'this is a string'

>>> s

'this is a string'

>>> s.upper()

'THIS IS A STRING'

>>> s.lower()

'this is a string'

>>> s = 'This Is A String'

>>> s

'This Is A String'

>>> s.swapcase()

'tHIS iS a sTRING'

>>> s

'This Is A String'
```

```
>>> s = 'this is a string'

>>> s.find('is')

2

>>>
</code>
```

Let us write some more string methods. You can do almost everything with these methods. You can use upper(), lower(), strip(), replace, find(), and many more.

```
<code>
#!/usr/bin/python3
s = 'this is a string'
print(s.find('is'))
newstring = s.replace('this', 'that')
print(newstring)
UpperString = s.upper()
print(UpperString)
# string is mutable, so id has been changed for the same string
print(id(s))
print(id(UpperString))
a = 'this is string with lot of whitespace at the beginning and at the end'
# by default it removes white space from start and end
RemovingWhiteSpace = a.strip()
print(RemovingWhiteSpace)
print(RemovingWhiteSpace.strip('this'))
</code>
```

In the above code, we first find out the position of "is" and it comes out as 2. Why? Because the first word is "this" and the sequence of the character starts as 0, 1, 2, and onwards. So at the position 0 there is "t", next at position 1 there is "h", and in the position 2 there is "i", and it starts reading from there.

Remember, string is mutable. So for the same string content the "ID" changes. We have seen that in our code.

Finally, in this code block we see an important function: strip(). By default it strips out whitespace from the beginning and the end. Otherwise, you need to provide the character you want to strip from the sentence.

```
<blockquote>
2
that is a string
THIS IS A STRING
140141176379480
140141176379768
```

this is string with lot of whitespace at the beginning and at the end
 is string with lot of whitespace at the beginning and at the end
</blockquote>

Consider this code:

```
<code>
x, y = 10, 11
f = "this {} is added and thereafter we add {}"
FormattedString = f.format(x, y)
print(FormattedString)
# we could have written it in C style
m, n = 10, 11
f = "this %d is added and thereafter we add %d"
FormattedString = f % (x, y)
print(FormattedString)
</code>
```

The output is the same.

</blockquote>
this 10 is added and thereafter we add 11
this 10 is added and thereafter we add 11
</blockquote>

But the difference is, in the latter part we have used Python 2 style. In that style, we format in "C" style and mention what kind of value we want to format. Here we wanted to format "decimal", so we have written "%d".

From Python 3.1 onwards this style has been changed, because this **wrapper of two curly braces, "{}",** and the **format()** function do the magic. Now you need not mention the value anymore. Before that, you had to mention the value you wanted to format. So more freedom and power are being added.

Look how we can format a dictionary value in our string:

```
<code>
a, b = 10, 11
s = "This is {}, and that is {}"
FormattedStirng = s.format(a, b)
print(FormattedStirng)
# we change the position
FormattedStirng = s.format(b, a)
print(FormattedStirng)
s = "This is {0}, and that is {1} and this too is {0} and that too is {1}"
FormattedStirng = s.format(a, b)
print(FormattedStirng)
# we can change it according to our wish with the positional argument
s = "This is {1}, and that is {1} and this too is {0} and that too is {1}"
```

```
FormattedStirng = s.format(a, b)
print(FormattedStirng)
# we can use it as dictionary
s = "This is {mine}, and that is {your} and this too is {your} and that too
is {mine}"
FormattedStirng = s.format(mine = a, your = b)
print(FormattedStirng)
# more dictionary staff
s = "This is my wish: {mine}, and that is your wish :{your} and this too is
mine: {mine} and that too is mine: {mine}"
FormattedStirng = s.format(mine = "I want to remove 'I'", your = "Do you
want to remove 'yourself'?")
print(FormattedStirng)
</code>
```

And here is the output:

<blockquote>
```
This is 10, and that is 11
This is 11, and that is 10
This is 10, and that is 11 and this too is 10 and that too is 11
This is 11, and that is 11 and this too is 10 and that too is 11
This is 10, and that is 11 and this too is 11 and that too is 10
This is my wish: I want to remove 'I', and that is your wish :Do you want to
remove 'yourself'? and this too is mine: I want to remove 'I' and that too
is mine: I want to remove 'I'
</blockquote>
```

How can we test that the string is immutable?

```
<code>
strings = "This is a string"
print(type(strings))
print(id(strings))
AnotherStrings = "This is a string"
print(type(AnotherStrings))
print(id(AnotherStrings))
print(strings.split())
words = strings.split()
words.append("and that ia also a string.")
print(type(words))
print(words[0])
NewWords = ":".join(words)
print(NewWords)
NewWords = ",".join(words)
print(NewWords)
words[0] = "That"
```

```
print(words)
</code>
```

<blockquote>

<class 'str'>
139956209543256
<class 'str'>
139956209543256
['This', 'is', 'a', 'string']
<class 'list'>
This
This:is:a:string:and that ia also a string.
This,is,a,string,and that ia also a string.
['That', 'is', 'a', 'string', 'and that ia also a string.']

</blockquote>

■ ■ ■

## CHAPTER 17

File Input And Output

Python has some built-in functions for dealing with files. You can open a file and read what is inside. You can write a file. That file could be a text file or a picture.

Each time we use the open() method and pass the mode as an argument. For reading a file we write "r" and for write we use "w". Let us consider a code where in an object we read a file and write it on another file using another object in the next step.

```
<code>
infile = open('files.txt', 'r')
outfile = open('new.txt', 'w')
for line in infile:
    print(line, file=outfile)
print("Done")
</code>
```

If we copy this way the file size is increased in the new text file. Now we have a comparatively large file. "Files.txt" is now "5.4 KB" and the "new.txt" is only 134 bytes.

If we copy by the old way the new file becomes "5.7 KB", a little bit larger than the former one. But Python has the technique to copy by buffer so that the buffer size remains intact.

Now we are going to write the contents of "files.txt" into "new.txt", but not by the old way. The new code is:

```
<code>
BufferSize = 500000
infile = open('files.txt', 'r')
outfile = open('new.txt', 'w')
buffer = infile.read(BufferSize)
while len(buffer):
    outfile.write(buffer)
    print("It is copying, it might take some time...please wait....",
    end='')
    buffer = infile.read(BufferSize)
print()
print("Copying Done.")
</code>
```

The output is as expected.

```
<blockquote>
It is copying, it might take some time...please wait....
Copying Done.
</blockquote>
```

Reading and writing binary file is the same. All you need to do is change the mode from "r" to "rb" and change the mode from "w" to "wb". That's it. Your code looks like this:

```
BufferSize = 5000000
infile = open('home.jpg', 'rb')
outfile = open('newimageofHome.jpg', 'wb')
buffer = infile.read(BufferSize)
while len(buffer):
    outfile.write(buffer)
    print("It is copying an image, it might take some time...please
    wait....", end='')
    buffer = infile.read(BufferSize)
print()
print("Copying Done.")
</code>
```

CHAPTER 18

■ ■ ■

Containers

In Python tuples and lists are array types. Tuples are immutable but lists are mutable. Tuples are used with comma operator and you can iterate through the tuple quite easily. As tuples are immutable, you can not add or update the value of a tuple. In lists, you can update or add new values quite easily. Open up your terminal in Linux and IDLE in Windows. Write down the code below and see the output yourself. Please read the comments that are attached with the code.

```
<code>
#!/usr/bin/python3
tuples1 = 1, 2, 3, 4
print(type(tuples1))
print(id(tuples1))
tuples2 = (1, 2, 3, 4)
print(type(tuples2))
print(id(tuples2))
print(tuples1[0])
print(tuples2[0])
# it will give the last item
print(tuples2[-1])
print(type(tuples1[0]))
print(type(tuples2[0]))
print(id(tuples1[0]))
print(id(tuples2[0]))
# tuple is immutable we can not change any value
# 'tuple' object does not support item assignment
# tuples2[0] = 120
# print(tuples2)
# to make an integer tuple you need to add comma separator
IsItTuple = (1)
print(type(IsItTuple))
IsItTuple = (1,)
print(type(IsItTuple))
# let us see how list behaves
list1 = [1, 2, 3, 4]
print(type(list1))
```

```
print(id(list1))
# first item
print(list1[0])
# last item
print(list1[-1])
# we can change the value of a list item
list1[0] = 120
print(list1) # output: [120, 2, 3, 4]
</code>
```

The output is like this:

```
<blockquote>
<class 'tuple'>
139794725901080
<class 'tuple'>
139794725900920
1
1
4
<class 'int'>
<class 'int'>
10455040
10455040
<class 'int'>
<class 'tuple'>
<class 'list'>
139794725273480
1
4
[120, 2, 3, 4]
</blockquote>
```

Operating on Tuple and List Object

Let us open up our terminal and test how tuples and lists work together.

```
<code>
root@kali:~# python3
Python 3.4.4 (default, Jan  5 2016, 15:35:18)
[GCC 5.3.1 20160101] on linux
Type "help", "copyright", "credits" or "license" for more information.
>>> t = (1,2,3,4)
>>> t
(1, 2, 3, 4)
>>> t[0]
1
```

```
>>> t = tuple(range(25))
>>> type(t)
<class 'tuple'>
>>> 50 in t
False
>>> 10 in t
True
>>> for i in t:print(i)
...
0
1
2
3
4
5
6
7
8
9
10
11
12
13
14
15
16
17
18
19
20
21
22
23
24
>>> l = list(range(20))
>>> type(l)
<class 'list'>
>>> for i in l:
... print(i)
  File "<stdin>", line 2
    print(i)
        ^
IndentationError: expected an indented block
>>> for i in l:print(i)
...
0
1
```

```
2
3
4
5
6
7
8
9
10
11
12
13
14
15
16
17
18
19
>>> l[2]
2
>>> 50 in l
False
>>> 12 in l
True
>>> t[0] = 25
Traceback (most recent call last):
  File "<stdin>", line 1, in <module>
TypeError: 'tuple' object does not support item assignment
>>> l[0] = 25
>>> print(l)
[25, 1, 2, 3, 4, 5, 6, 7, 8, 9, 10, 11, 12, 13, 14, 15, 16, 17, 18, 19]
>>> t.append(50)
Traceback (most recent call last):
  File "<stdin>", line 1, in <module>
AttributeError: 'tuple' object has no attribute 'append'
>>> l.append(120)
>>> print(l
l        lambda    len(     license( list(     locals(
>>> print(l)
[25, 1, 2, 3, 4, 5, 6, 7, 8, 9, 10, 11, 12, 13, 14, 15, 16, 17, 18, 19, 120]
>>> t.count()
Traceback (most recent call last):
  File "<stdin>", line 1, in <module>
TypeError: count() takes exactly one argument (0 given)
>>> t.count(5)
1
>>> l.append(25)
```

```
>>> l.count(25)
2
>>> t.index(10)
10
>>> l.index(10)
10
>>> l.extend(range(25))
>>> for i in l:print(i)
...
25
1
2
3
4
5
6
7
8
9
10
11
12
13
14
15
16
17
18
19
120
25
0
1
2
3
4
5
6
7
8
9
10
11
12
13
14
15
```

```
16
17
18
19
20
21
22
23
24
>>> l.insert(0, 4656)
>>> l[0]
4656
>>> l.insert(12, 147)
>>> l.index(12)
14
>>> l[12]
147
>>> l.remove(12)
>>> l[12]
147
>>> print(l)
[4656, 25, 1, 2, 3, 4, 5, 6, 7, 8, 9, 10, 147, 11, 13, 14, 15, 16, 17, 18,
19, 120, 25, 0, 1, 2, 3, 4, 5, 6, 7, 8, 9, 10, 11, 12, 13, 14, 15, 16, 17,
18, 19, 20, 21, 22, 23, 24]
>>> l.remove(12)
>>> print(l)
[4656, 25, 1, 2, 3, 4, 5, 6, 7, 8, 9, 10, 147, 11, 13, 14, 15, 16, 17, 18,
19, 120, 25, 0, 1, 2, 3, 4, 5, 6, 7, 8, 9, 10, 11, 13, 14, 15, 16, 17, 18,
19, 20, 21, 22, 23, 24]
>>> l.pop(0)
4656
>>> print(l)
[25, 1, 2, 3, 4, 5, 6, 7, 8, 9, 10, 147, 11, 13, 14, 15, 16, 17, 18, 19,
120, 25, 0, 1, 2, 3, 4, 5, 6, 7, 8, 9, 10, 11, 13, 14, 15, 16, 17, 18, 19,
20, 21, 22, 23, 24]
>>> l.pop()
24
>>> print(l)
[25, 1, 2, 3, 4, 5, 6, 7, 8, 9, 10, 147, 11, 13, 14, 15, 16, 17, 18, 19,
120, 25, 0, 1, 2, 3, 4, 5, 6, 7, 8, 9, 10, 11, 13, 14, 15, 16, 17, 18, 19,
20, 21, 22, 23]
>>>
</code>
```

Write down the same code and see how it works in your machine. Errors may come out as happened in the above code. But remember, each error will help you to learn a few new things.

Operating on Dictionary Object

As you have tested tuples and lists, you can test the dictionary object and see how it works.

```
<code>
root@kali:~# python3
Python 3.4.4 (default, Jan  5 2016, 15:35:18)
[GCC 5.3.1 20160101] on linux
Type "help", "copyright", "credits" or "license" for more information.
>>> x = {'one':1, 'two':2, 'three':3}
>>> type(x)
<class 'dict'>
>>> y = dict(four = 4, five = 5, six = 6)
>>> type(y)
<class 'dict'>
>>> z = dict(seven = 7, eight = 8, nine = 9, **x, **y)
  File "<stdin>", line 1
    z = dict(seven = 7, eight = 8, nine = 9, **x, **y)
                                               ^
SyntaxError: invalid syntax
>>> z = dict(seven = 7, eight = 8, nine = 9, **x)
>>> type(z)
<class 'dict'>
>>> print(z)
{'eight': 8, 'two': 2, 'nine': 9, 'one': 1, 'seven': 7, 'three': 3}
>>> for i in z:print(i)
...
eight
two
nine
one
seven
three
>>> for key, value in z.items():print(key, value)
...
eight 8
two 2
nine 9
one 1
seven 7
three 3
>>> for key, value in z.items():
...    if key == two:
...        print(value)
...
```

```
Traceback (most recent call last):
  File "<stdin>", line 2, in <module>
NameError: name 'two' is not defined
>>> z.pop()
Traceback (most recent call last):
  File "<stdin>", line 1, in <module>
TypeError: pop expected at least 1 arguments, got 0
>>> z.pop(three)
Traceback (most recent call last):
  File "<stdin>", line 1, in <module>
NameError: name 'three' is not defined
>>> z.pop('three')
3
>>> for i in z:print(i)
...
eight
two
nine
one
seven
>>> for key, value in z.items():
...    if key == 'nine':
...        print(value)
...
9
>>>
</code>
```

The more you spend time with tuples, lists, and dictionaries, the more you learn about Python. There are a lot of built-in functions and you can use those functions quite easily to get more out of your code. Another key concept of dictionary is "key=>value" pair. As you progress further and learn more languages along with Python, you will find that each language uses this concept, taking it further to solve major problems. The web frameworks, in particular, use this concept very heavily.

CHAPTER 19

Database

Database operations in Python are fairly simple. For the small amount of work, the built-in SQLite3 is quite competitive. You can easily maintain it by creating, retrieving and updating and deleting it.

The basic term is "CRUD." "C" stands for create, "R" stands for retrieve, "U" for update, and "D" for delete. With any database you generally perform these actions.

Let us start with SQLite3.

There is a large library inside the Python home. All the functions and properties of SQLite3 are stored there, so you can easily import them and use them for your project. Consider this code:

```
<code>
#!/usr/bin/python3
import sqlite3
def main():
    db = sqlite3.connect('test.db')
    db.row_factory = sqlite3.Row
    db.execute('drop table if exists test1')
    db.execute('create table test1 (t1 text, i1 int)')
    db.execute('insert into test1 (t1, i1) values (?, ?)', ('Babu', 1))
    db.execute('insert into test1 (t1, i1) values (?, ?)', ('Mana', 2))
    db.execute('insert into test1 (t1, i1) values (?, ?)', ('Bappa', 3))
    db.execute('insert into test1 (t1, i1) values (?, ?)', ('Babua', 4))
    db.execute('insert into test1 (t1, i1) values (?, ?)', ('Anju', 5))
    db.execute('insert into test1 (t1, i1) values (?, ?)', ('Patai', 6))
    db.execute('insert into test1 (t1, i1) values (?, ?)', ('GasaBuddhu', 7))
    db.execute('insert into test1 (t1, i1) values (?, ?)', ('Tapas', 8))
    db.commit()
    DatabaseRead = db.execute('select * from test order by i1')
    for row in DatabaseRead:
        # print(dict(row))
        print(row['t1'])
        # print(row['t1'], row['i1'])
```

```
    # print(type(row))
if __name__ == "__main__":main()
</code>
```

If you run this code, you will see a list of names I just added. As you see, we have connected with a database, "test". Next we added a table with two columns. The first column is the id integer and we keep the ID of each name inside it. The second column is the placeholder of text. We keep a few names there.

You can write the same code and test it. It will give you the same result. Once you run the code, you will find that a file "test.db" has been created inside your project.

MySQL for Big Project

SQLite3 is good for a small amount of work. But for a big project, it is better to opt for a database like MySQL. To work with MySQL in Python3 you need to download and install MySQL connector. The download and installation part is quite easy.

In Python2* you can by default import MySQL Connector. But for Python3, you need to download the file. Open https://python.org and search for MySQL Connector. Download the file and run "setup.py".

Once you download and install the MySQL Connector module it is fairly simple and easy to connect to any MySQL database.

Consider this code where we simply connect to a MySQL database and have a printout "connected."

If MySQL or any database operation is completely new to you, it is better to learn about the simple database operations and database query language. In Windows or Linux, installing PHPMyAdmin is very easy. Just install it and you need not write all the SQL code to build a database and all the tables.

Let us assume that we have a database called "python-mysql". In that database we have some tables. Now we are going to connect to that database first.

```
<code>
#!/usr/bin/python3
import mysql.connector
from mysql.connector import Error
def ConnectionTest():
### connecting to MySQL Database ###
    try:
        ### you can either use a dictionary object or you can connect
        directly ###
        ### using a dictioanry connection object ###
        kwargs = dict(host = 'localhost', database = 'python_mysql',
        user = 'root', password = 'pass')
        conn = mysql.connector.connect(**kwargs)
        ### connecting directly ###
        connection = mysql.connector.connect(host = 'localhost',
                                             database = 'python_mysql',
                                             user = 'root',
                                             password = 'pass')
```

```
        if conn.is_connected():
            print("Connected from 'conn' object")
    except Error as e:
        print(e)
    finally:
        connection.close()
if __name__ == "__main__":
    ConnectionTest()
</code>
```

It will give us a printout "Connected from a conn object". It means the databse connection has been set up. Now it is time to retrieve the value from the table.

In this database we have two tables. One is of "authors" and the other is "books". MySQL Connector class has all the functions needed to perform any task to those tables. You can fetch all the records. You can decide how many books or how many authors you would like to fetch. The following code shows you both. But a few parts have been commented out.

To test this code you need to have a database first. Name it "python-mysql". Next you need to have two tables called "authors" and "books". You also need to fill up those tables. It is always better to search online and download a ready-made MySQL database and tables. They are available. It is highly suggested that you search for MySQL Connector and see what you find.

In the following code, please go through the commented sections also. That says a lot about how you can retrieve your records and show them to the world.

```
<code>
#!/usr/bin/python3
import mysql.connector
from mysql.connector import Error
def RetrieveValues():
    try:
        kwargs = dict(host = 'localhost', database = 'python_mysql', user =
        'root', password = 'pass')
        conn = mysql.connector.connect(**kwargs)
        ### shows you how to query data from a MySQL database in Python by using
        MySQL Connector/Python API
        # such as fetchone() , fetchmany() , and fetchall() ###
        if conn.is_connected():
            cursors = conn.cursor()
            cursors.execute('SELECT * FROM authors')
            # row = cursors.fetchone()
            # output (1, 'Bel and the Dragon ', '123828863494')
            ######
            # now we try to get all the books
            # row = cursors.fetchall()
            # print(type(row))
            # output <class 'list'>, so we can use for loop
            # for books in row:
```

```
            # print(books)
            # it will give us list of all the books
            ######
            ### now we give the size of how many books we want to get ###
            # HowManyBooks = 8
            # row = cursors.fetchmany(HowManyBooks)
            # for books in row:
            # print(books)
            # we get the output of 8 books
            row = cursors.fetchall()
            for books in row:
                print(books)
    except Error as e:
        print(e)
    finally: conn.close()
if __name__ == "__main__":
    RetrieveValues()
</code>
```

We have used the try and error method so that if connection fails, it would not show an ugly "Error" message on your project. Second, this method is quite direct. You can also use a configuration file to do the same thing.

It is strongly advisable to use a configuration file (we say "config file"). The configuration file has all the things necessary to connect to the database.

We can write in the configuration file like this and save it as "mysql_config.ini".

```
<code>
[mysql]
host = localhost
database = YourDatabaseName
user = root
password = pass
</code>
```

Let us see how this ".ini" file can be parsed through our Python code. We save this file as "MySQL_Connector.py".

```
<code>
#!/usr/bin/python3
from configparser import ConfigParser
def ReadingMySQLConfig(filemame = 'mysql_config.ini', section = 'mysql'):
    parser = ConfigParser()
    parser.read(filemame)
    db = dict()
    if parser.has_section(section):
        items = parser.items(section)
        for item in items:
            db[item[0]] = item[1]
```

```
        else:
                raise Exception('{0} not found in the {1} file'.format(section,
filename))
        return db
</code>
```

You see that we have imported the necessary modules for parsing the configuration file and finally we have used that configuration file to connect to the database. And in the above code of "MySQL_Connector.py" we have included that "mysql_config.ini" file in this line—**def ReadingMySQLConfig(filename = 'mysql_config.ini', section = 'mysql'):**—as an argument.

How we can use this configuration file to test our connection is shown below.

```
<code>
#!/usr/bin/python3
from mysql.connector import MySQLConnection, Error
from MySQL_Connector.mysql_config import ReadingMySQLConfig
def Connect():
    kwargs = ReadingMySQLConfig()
    MyConnection = MySQLConnection(**kwargs)
    try:
        if MyConnection.is_connected():
            print("Connected")
    except Error as e:
        print(e)
    finally:
        MyConnection.close()
if __name__ == "__main__":
    Connect()
</code>
```

Now we have decoupled our code more. We are able to divide it in small segments so that our connection code looks extremely small and organized. But you can always connect to your MySQL database like below.

```
<code>
#!/usr/bin/python3
# -*- coding: utf-8 -*-
import mysql.connector
from mysql.connector import Error
def connect():
    """ Connect to MySQL database """
    try:
        conn = mysql.connector.connect(host='localhost',
                                       database='YourDatabase',
                                       user='root',
                                       password='YourPassword')
```

141

```
        if conn.is_connected():
            print('Connected to MySQL database')
    except Error as e:
        print(e)
    finally:
        conn.close()
if __name__ == '__main__':
    connect()
</code>
```

Now the time has come to retrieve records from the database. We are able to connect to the database. Now, there should not be any trouble fetching records from the tables of the database. We have two built-in methods in our Python library. The methods are "fetchmany()" and "fetchall()". The first method, "fetchmany()", gives you the liberty to decide how many rows you are going to fetch. Let us see the code:

```
//query with fetchmany()
<code>
#!/usr/bin/python3
from mysql.connector import MySQLConnection, Error
from Databases.python_mysql_dbconfig import read_db_config
def iter_row(cursor, size=10):
    while True:
        rows = cursor.fetchmany(size)
        if not rows:
            break
        for row in rows:
            yield row
def query_with_fetchmany():
    try:
        dbconfig = read_db_config()
        conn = MySQLConnection(**dbconfig)
        cursor = conn.cursor()
        cursor.execute("SELECT * FROM EMPLOYEE")
# EMPLOYEE is the table name
        for row in iter_row(cursor, 10):
            print(row)
    except Error as e:
        print(e)
    finally:
        cursor.close()
        conn.close()
if __name__ == '__main__':
    query_with_fetchmany()
</code>
```

The method "fetchall()" brings all the records from a table.

```
<code>
#!/usr/bin/python3
from mysql.connector import MySQLConnection, Error
from Databases.python_mysql_dbconfig import read_db_config
def query_with_fetchall():
    try:
        dbconfig = read_db_config()
        conn = MySQLConnection(**dbconfig)
        cursor = conn.cursor()
        cursor.execute("SELECT * FROM EMPLOYEE")
        rows = cursor.fetchall()
        print('Total Row(s):', cursor.rowcount)
        for row in rows:
            print("First Name = ", row[0])
            print("Second Name = ", row[1])
            print("Age = ", row[2])
            print("Sex = ", row[3])
            print("Salary = ", row[4])
    except Error as e:
        print(e)
    finally:
        cursor.close()
        conn.close()
if __name__ == '__main__':
    query_with_fetchall()
</code>
```

You see how we can fetch the records as our requirements. Now let us try to test the insertion process. In our CRUD application, the first "C" stands for "Create." Here the word "Create" means nothing but insertion of new records. Through MySQL Connector it is quite simple. All you need is that the connection must be on. After that you need to insert your records.

Here is the code. We have a "Book" table in our database and we are going to insert two records into it. One is the title of the book and the other is the ISBN code of the book.

```
<code>
#!/usr/bin/python3
from mysql.connector import MySQLConnection, Error
from MySQL_Connector.mysql_config import ReadingMySQLConfig
def InsertBooks(books):
    query = "INSERT INTO books(title, isbn) VALUES(%s, %s)"
    try:
        kwargs = ReadingMySQLConfig()
        MyConnection = MySQLConnection(**kwargs)
        if MyConnection.is_connected():
            cursor = MyConnection.cursor()
```

```
            cursor.executemany(query, books)
            MyConnection.commit()
    except Error as e:
        print(e)
    finally:
        MyConnection.close()
def main():
    books = [("TestBook", 1236547890)]
    InsertBooks(books)
    print("Inserted one book")
if __name__ == "__main__":
    main()
</code>
```

We have successfully inserted one book title and ISBN code. The next process will be updating that title and ISBN code. That is also very easy. All you need is the unique ID of the book. Once you have provided the unique ID of the book, you can update it easily.

```
<ocde>
#!/usr/bin/python3
from mysql.connector import MySQLConnection, Error
from MySQL_Connector.mysql_config import ReadingMySQLConfig
def UpdateBooks(book_id, title):
    kwargs = ReadingMySQLConfig()
    data = (title, book_id)
    query = "UPDATE books SET title = %s WHERE id = %s"
    try:
        MyConnection = MySQLConnection(**kwargs)
        cursor = MyConnection.cursor()
        cursor.execute(query, data)
        MyConnection.commit()
    except Error as e:
        print(e)
    finally:
        MyConnection.close()
def main():
    for id in range(1, 25):
        if id == 3:
            UpdateBooks(id, "I Have A Dream")
            print("One book has been updated")
        elif id == 4:
            UpdateBooks(id, "Laravel 5 Unfolded")
            print("One book has been updated")
        elif id == 5:
            UpdateBooks(id, "Play With Python")
            print("One book has been updated")
if __name__ == "__main__":
    main()
</code>
```

We have successfully updated three books which have unique IDs of 3, 4, and 5, respectively. Finally we will see how we can delete a record.

To delete a record, once again you need the unique ID.

```python
#!/usr/bin/python3
from mysql.connector import MySQLConnection, Error
from MySQL_Connector.mysql_config import ReadingMySQLConfig
def DeleteBooks(book_id):
    kwargs = ReadingMySQLConfig()
    query = "DELETE FROM books WHERE id = %s"
    try:
        MyConnection = MySQLConnection(**kwargs)
        cursor = MyConnection.cursor()
        cursor.execute(query, (book_id,))
        MyConnection.commit()
    except Error as e:
        print(e)
    finally:
        MyConnection.close()
def main():
    id = 87
    DeleteBooks(id)
    print("Deleted ", id, "number of book from books")
if __name__ == "__main__":
    main()
```

In this code, this line—"**cursor.execute(query, (book_id,))**"—is extremely important. You probably notice that we have used a "," separator after the "book_id". It is your task to find out why this comma separator has been used. The only clue is it is related to either "tuples" or "lists". It is your task that you find out what is the actual reason.

Like every modern version of relational databases, MySQL also allows you to keep a binary large object inside it. Normally when you write numbers or strings they do not take up much space. But what about the images? Let us assume that we have an author table where we need to keep images for the authors. We may also want to keep the cover pictures of the books in our book table.

Normally this image or any binary large object is called, in short, "BLOB". Let us update our author table with an image and see how it works.

```python
#!/usr/bin/python3
from mysql.connector import MySQLConnection, Error
from MySQL_Connector.mysql_config import ReadingMySQLConfig
def ReadFile(filename):
    with open(filename, 'rb') as f:
        images = f.read()
```

```
    return images
def UpdateImage(author_id, filename):
    kwargs = ReadingMySQLConfig()
    data = ReadFile(filename)
    query = "UPDATE authors SET photo = %s WHERE id = %s"
    args = (data, author_id)
    try:
        MyConnection = MySQLConnection(**kwargs)
        cursor = MyConnection.cursor()
        cursor.execute(query, args)
        MyConnection.commit()
    except Error as e:
        print(e)
    finally:
        MyConnection.close()
def main():
    id = 47
    UpdateImage(id, "/home/hagudu/Pictures/ss.jpg")
    print("Image of author ID", id, "has been updated.")
if __name__ == "__main__":
    main()
</code>
```

The code is fairly simple. At least at this stage you should find it simple. The steps are like this:

1. Read the file with the help of the "with" keyword and store it in a variable and return it. We pass the parameter through the function. See the first function: "ReadFile(filename)".

2. The second function is crucial because it passes the same file name as one of the parameters. It also connects to the database and commits. See the second function: "UpdateImage(author_id, filename)".

3. Finally, we call the second function and pass the path of the image file as an argument so that our Python code reaches there and retrieves the image by opening it and finally committing to the database.

Now we are going to retrieve one image from the database and write it on our local disk. In the previous code we have read the file. Now it is time to write the file on our disk. The code is almost similar except for a few changes.

```
<code>
#!/usr/bin/python3
from mysql.connector import MySQLConnection, Error
from MySQL_Connector.mysql_config import ReadingMySQLConfig
def WriteFile(data, filename):
    with open(filename, 'wb') as files:
        files.write(data)
def ReadImage(author_id, filename):
    kwargs = ReadingMySQLConfig()
    query = 'SELECT photo FROM authors WHERE id = %s'
    try:
        MyConnection = MySQLConnection(**kwargs)
        cursor = MyConnection.cursor()
        cursor.execute(query, (author_id,))
        photo = cursor.fetchone()[0]
        WriteFile(photo, filename)
    except Error as e:
        print(e)
    finally:
        MyConnection.close()
def main():
    id = 47
    ReadImage(id, "/home/hagudu/Pictures/ss1.jpg")
if __name__ == "__main__":
    main()
</code>
```

CHAPTER 20

Module

In Python when you leave the shell or terminal or Python interpreter, the script is lost. After all, you don't write programs to lose at the end of the day. It may be a simple calculator program. But you want to use it again. Another important thing is you need to use your one code in your other code. You may want to use other people's code also.

To solve this dilemma, the concept of "module" comes in.

You write a simple calculator program and save the file as "cal.py". If you are in the root directory of your project you can easily use your calculator in your other program. Once you write a Python code and save it with a name, that name becomes a module.

In this case, "cal" becomes a module. Now you can "import" that "cal" module into any other code or module. In the large Python library there are tons of modules. You can always import them and use them. Consider the code below. In this code we have imported three modules. The first is "sys" or system-specific module. The second one is "os" or operating system–specific module and the third one is "urllib" which means a library that is URL-specific. You notice that we write `"urllib.request"`. The "dot" notation means we actually call something called "request" from the Python URL library. Actually, the web architecture primarily depends upon two things: request and respond. Here we are going to request something from a URL.

```
<code>
#!/usr/bin/python3
import sys, os, urllib.request
def main():
    print("This is Python Version : {}.{}.{}".format(*sys.version_info))
    # os module
    print(os.name)
    print(os.getenv('PATH'))
    print(os.getcwd())

    #urllib module
    page = urllib.request.urlopen('http://arshinagar.in/')
    for line in page:
        print(str(line, encoding='utf-8'), end='')
if __name__ == "__main__":
    main()
</code>
```

You see that in the first part of the code we have used the "sys" module and wanted to know the version of Python our system is using. The second part is all about the operating system. It gives us the name, path, and many other things. And in the last part we are requesting a web page.

Let us see the output in a Linux Debian distribution like Ubuntu first. The first line is the version and the second line is about the operating system, which is "posix". The third line is the environment path and the fourth line is the actual path where this file is stored.

From the fifth line you see the "urllib.request" starts working in and fetches the whole index page from a web site. I have used my friend's web site. I do not print out the whole HTML output, as it would take lots of space. Go through each line and see how different modules work.

```
<blockquote>
This is Python Version : 3.4.3
posix
/usr/local/sbin:/usr/local/bin:/usr/sbin:/usr/bin:/sbin:/bin:/usr/games:/
usr/local/games
/home/hagudu/PycharmProjects/FirstPythonProject/modules
<!DOCTYPE html>
<html  lang="en">
<head>
<meta charset="UTF-8" />
<meta name="viewport" content="width=device-width" />
<meta name="viewport" content="initial-scale=1.0" />
<meta name="HandheldFriendly" content="true"/>
<link rel="profile" href="http://gmpg.org/xfn/11" />
<link rel="pingback" href="http://www.arshinagar.in/xmlrpc.php" />
<title>Arshinagar &#8211; Just another WordPress site</title>
<link rel="alternate" type="application/rss+xml" title="Arshinagar &raquo;
Feed" href="http://www.arshinagar.in/feed/" />
<link rel="alternate" type="application/rss+xml" title="Arshinagar &raquo;
Comments Feed" href="http://www.arshinagar.in/comments/feed/" />
//the details are removed for brevity
Process finished with exit code 0
</blockquote>
```

Now we can try this same code in Windows and compare the output.

```
<blockquote>
This is Python Version : 3.4.4
nt
C:\WINDOWS\system32;C:\WINDOWS;C:\WINDOWS\System32\Wbem;C:\Program Files\
Microsoft SQL Server\90\Tools\binn\
D:\pthon-files-fromwindows
</blockquote>
```

In this output you see the Python version has been changed. The operating system is not "posix" anymore. It is "nt" now. The environment path and the file path are also poles apart. I removed the "urllib.request" module output for concision.

We can see more module examples here.

```
<code>
#!/usr/bin/python3
import sys, os, urllib.request, random, datetime
def main():
    print("This is Python Version : {}.{}.{}".format(*sys.version_info))

    # random module
    print(random.randint(1, 1000))
    x = list(range(25))
    print(x)
    random.shuffle(x)
    print(x)
    random.shuffle(x)
    print(x)
    random.shuffle(x)
    print(x)
    PresentTime = datetime.datetime.now()
    print(PresentTime)
    print(PresentTime.year, PresentTime.month, PresentTime.day, PresentTime.
    hour, PresentTime.minute, PresentTime.second, PresentTime.microsecond)

if __name__ == "__main__":
    main()
</code>
```

In this code we add two more modules. They are "random" and "datetime". We get the output below to see how they work.

```
</blockquote>
This is Python Version : 3.4.3
366
[0, 1, 2, 3, 4, 5, 6, 7, 8, 9, 10, 11, 12, 13, 14, 15, 16, 17, 18, 19, 20,
21, 22, 23, 24]
[23, 6, 22, 3, 7, 19, 10, 16, 8, 12, 15, 21, 11, 17, 9, 13, 4, 14, 24, 18,
0, 2, 1, 20, 5]
[0, 8, 21, 5, 13, 3, 2, 18, 24, 12, 4, 19, 14, 17, 20, 10, 11, 22, 15, 9, 6,
23, 1, 7, 16]
[11, 6, 23, 14, 9, 7, 3, 5, 15, 2, 19, 0, 16, 24, 21, 12, 4, 13, 22, 20, 10,
8, 1, 17, 18]
//here is the output of date and time module
2016-03-23 08:34:37.253888
2016 3 23 8 34 37 253888
</blockquote>
```

Each time you run the code, you get a new number as the "random" module always produces new numbers. To get more ideas, you need to go through the Python Standard Library in the official Python web site or download the Python 3.4.4 documentation. It is available in many file types, including simple text file or PDF. The "datetime" module page in Python Standard Library in the documentation looks like this:

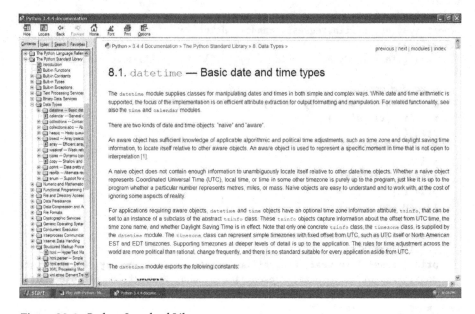

Figure 20-1. *Python Standard Library*

Now you can go back to your old codes and see them again in a new light. Now you will easily understand why we have used the MySQL Connector module or Configuration Parser module.

CHAPTER 21

■ ■ ■

Debugging, Unittest Module

Now you have progressed a lot. In the process of coding you must have found or seen many types of errors. It is quite obvious. The seasoned programmers also make mistakes. You have also learned to catch your errors. But the situation may come when you need to update your code. It might happen. You need to modify or add a few lines in your code. It may either work or it may fail. In your new lines of code there could be "syntactical" errors. There could be "runtime" errors. Usually the Python interpreter tries to guide you in such cases. Generally it points out where the error has occurred. But not always.

In such cases the "unittest" module comes to your help.

In Python standard library you get a lot of information about this module. You may also search the Internet about the "nose" tool, which does something similar. The basic concept is, you have a code repository somewhere and you have a separate unit testing schedule. It is an automated test.

Suppose we have a folder called "MyTest/BrainAndSoul". Inside this folder we have a Python file called "saytimedate.py". It is a very simple file that will tell us the version of Python and the present time and date. To get that output, we need two modules: "sys" and "datetime". We have two methods to get those outputs. To get the output, all we need to do is call them under "main()" function. We do exactly that.

At the same time we have two separate methods that begin with the word "test". The methods are "test_PyVar()" and "test_main()".

```
<code>
#!/usr/bin/python3
# coding=utf-8
import sys, datetime
def PyVer():
    print("This is Python Version : {}.{}.{}".format(*sys.version_info))
def PyTime():
    PresentTime = datetime.datetime.now()
    print(PresentTime)
    print(PresentTime.year, PresentTime.month, PresentTime.day, PresentTime.
    hour, PresentTime.minute,
        PresentTime.second, PresentTime.microsecond)
    #print(obj)
def main():
    PyVer()
```

```
    PyTime()
def test_Pyvar():
    PyVer()
def test_Main():
    PyTime()
if __name__ == "__main__":
    main()
<code>
```

When you run this code, your main() function calls the two methods defined inside it. And the output below is what is expected.

```
</blockquote>
This is Python Version : 3.4.2
2016-04-22 23:30:30.435691
2016 4 22 23 30 30 435691
</blockquote>
```

Now, in a completely separate folder, we would like to run the "unittest" module and see whether this code passes or fails. Since we have already run the code and gotten a successful output, we can safely say that this code will pass the test.

The name of our unit testing code is "TestUnitTest.py" and the code looks like this:

```
<code>
#!/usr/bin/python3
# coding=utf-8
import MyProject.BrainAndSoul.saytimedate
import unittest
class SayTiemDate(unittest.TestCase):
    def setUP(self):
        pass
    def test_Version(self): self.assertEqual(MyProject.BrainAndSoul.
    saytimedate.PyVer(), MyProject.BrainAndSoul.saytimedate.test_Pyvar())

    def test_Time(self): self.assertEqual(MyProject.BrainAndSoul.
    saytimedate.main(), MyProject.BrainAndSoul.saytimedate.test_Main())

if __name__ == "__main__":
    unittest.main()
</code>
```

What does this code say? As you see, there are two methods: "test_Time()" and "test_Version()". We have not passed any argument. Both the methods call one default method from the "unittest" module. And that is "assertEqual()". Through this method we have passed two methods that we have defined earlier in the "MyTest/BrainAndSoul" folder. Inside that folder we have a Python file called "saytimedate.py". We are now comparing two methods through our "unittest" module.

Finally it gives a nice output like this if everything runs properly.

<blockquote>
Testing started at 8:58 PM ...
This is Python Version : 3.4.2
This is Python Version : 3.4.2
Process finished with exit code 0
</blockquote>

When you run the code it looks like the following image in your "PyCharm" IDE.

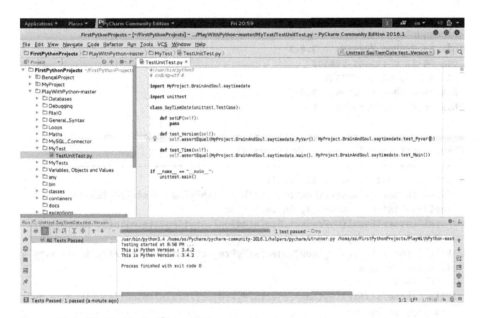

Figure 21-1. *Unittest in PyCharm IDE*

If we run that code again we may get an output like this:

<blockquote>
This is Python Version : 3.4.2
2016-04-23 05:47:23.608853
2016 4 23 5 47 23 608853
2016-04-23 05:47:23.608951
2016 4 23 5 47 23 608951
This is Python Version : 3.4.2
This is Python Version : 3.4.2
• •

</blockquote>

Ran 2 tests in 0.001s

OK

Process finished with exit code 0
</blockquote>

Now for testing purposes we change our source code and make some mistakes intentionally to see whether our "unittest" module fails or not.

If there is any error, the output will change and give an error message something like this:

<blockquote>
This is Python Version : 3.4.2
2016-04-23 05:51:45.994547
2016 4 23 5 51 45 994547
This is Python Version : 3.4.2
This is Python Version : 3.4.2
E.
==
ERROR: test_Time (__main__.SayTiemDate)
--
Traceback (most recent call last):
  File "/home/ss/FirstPythonProjects/PlayWithPython-master/MyTest/
  TestUnitTest.py", line 17, in test_Time
    self.assertEqual(MyProject.BrainAndSoul.saytimedate.main(), MyProject.
    BrainAndSoul.saytimedate.test_Main())
  File "/home/ss/FirstPythonProjects/MyProject/BrainAndSoul/saytimedate.py",
  line 20, in main
    PyTime()
  File "/home/ss/FirstPythonProjects/MyProject/BrainAndSoul/saytimedate.py",
  line 15, in PyTime
    print(obj)
NameError: name 'obj' is not defined

--
Ran 2 tests in 0.001s

FAILED (errors=1)

Process finished with exit code 1
</blockquote>

Now you can try to run more unit testing modules. Here is another example where the test is successful.

CHAPTER 22

Socket and Networking

This chapter is kind of an introduction to the advanced concepts of Python. Since this is the final chapter, I would like to tell you about where you can go from here.

You can either build web applications with the help of Python or you can do some security networking stuff. Finally, like me, you can choose the interesting path of ethical hacking. All these things and more you can do through Python.

Let us see how we can apply our basic knowledge of Python in socket and networking. Write down this code on your IDE and see what output you get.

```
<code>
# coding=utf-8
import socket
print(socket.gethostbyname("www.mesanjib.wordpress.com"))
print(socket.gethostbyname("www.sanjib.pythonanywhere.com"))

</code>
```

The output is like this in my machine. You can test any other web site to get its address. This is the tip of the iceberg. Lots of things are inside. It is better for you to see everything that is inside than for me to tell you, as I feel you should concentrate on trying to write basic concepts of Python more and more.

```
<blockquote>
192.0.78.12
50.19.109.98

Process finished with exit code 0
</blockquote>
```

In the further study of the relationship between ethical hacking and Python 3, you'll find these socket and networking concepts extremely useful.

Let us move further to Part Three of the book, where we'll learn about anonymity.

An ethical hacker should always remain anonymous.

Why? Let us see.

© Sanjib Sinha 2017

S. Sinha, *Beginning Ethical Hacking with Python*, DOI 10.1007/978-1-4842-2541-7_22

CHAPTER 23

■ ■ ■

Importing Nmap Module

Nmap (Network Mapper) is a security scanner. It was originally written by Gordon Lyon (also known by his pseudonym Fyodor Vaskovich). This tool is particularly used to discover hosts and services on a computer network. While finding the hosts and services it creates a "map" of the network. For this reasom it has been widely called 'Nmap' or you can also call it 'Network Mapper'. It is regarded as an essential tool in your pursuit to be a good and competent ethical hacker.

To get the best results, Nmap usually sends specially crafted packets to the target host and then analyzes the responses and finds what ports are open. It also assesses the vulnerability of a computer network.

This software widely used by the hackers has number of features. It actually probes computer networks, discovering hosts and services. It also detects operating system and it decides the vulnerability of the systems by finding the open ports.

Python actually extends these features so that you can easily do more advanced service detection, vulnerability detection and other things.

Let us first check whether 'Nmap' module of python has already been installed in our system or not by issuing a simple command on the terminal.

nmap

It gives us a long listing which is very important. Many things you can learn from this listing as it says about the version, usages and at the end it also says where you can get the manual for more reading.

```
Nmap 6.40 ( http://nmap.org )
Usage: nmap [Scan Type(s)] [Options] {target specification}
TARGET SPECIFICATION:
  Can pass hostnames, IP addresses, networks, etc.
  Ex: scanme.nmap.org, microsoft.com/24, 192.168.0.1; 10.0.0-255.1-254
  -iL <inputfilename>: Input from list of hosts/networks
  -iR <num hosts>: Choose random targets
  --exclude <host1[,host2][,host3],...>: Exclude hosts/networks
  --excludefile <exclude_file>: Exclude list from file
```

© Sanjib Sinha 2017
S. Sinha, *Beginning Ethical Hacking with Python*, DOI 10.1007/978-1-4842-2541-7_23

```
HOST DISCOVERY:
  -sL: List Scan - simply list targets to scan
  -sn: Ping Scan - disable port scan
  -Pn: Treat all hosts as online -- skip host discovery
  -PS/PA/PU/PY[portlist]: TCP SYN/ACK, UDP or SCTP discovery to given ports
  -PE/PP/PM: ICMP echo, timestamp, and netmask request discovery probes
  -PO[protocol list]: IP Protocol Ping
  -n/-R: Never do DNS resolution/Always resolve [default: sometimes]
  --dns-servers <serv1[,serv2],...>: Specify custom DNS servers
  --system-dns: Use OS's DNS resolver
  --traceroute: Trace hop path to each host
SCAN TECHNIQUES:
  -sS/sT/sA/sW/sM: TCP SYN/Connect()/ACK/Window/Maimon scans
  -sU: UDP Scan
  -sN/sF/sX: TCP Null, FIN, and Xmas scans
  --scanflags <flags>: Customize TCP scan flags
  -sI <zombie host[:probeport]>: Idle scan
  -sY/sZ: SCTP INIT/COOKIE-ECHO scans
  -sO: IP protocol scan
  -b <FTP relay host>: FTP bounce scan
PORT SPECIFICATION AND SCAN ORDER:
  -p <port ranges>: Only scan specified ports
    Ex: -p22; -p1-65535; -p U:53,111,137,T:21-25,80,139,8080,S:9
  -F: Fast mode - Scan fewer ports than the default scan
  -r: Scan ports consecutively - don't randomize
  --top-ports <number>: Scan <number> most common ports
  --port-ratio <ratio>: Scan ports more common than <ratio>
SERVICE/VERSION DETECTION:
  -sV: Probe open ports to determine service/version info
  --version-intensity <level>: Set from 0 (light) to 9 (try all probes)
  --version-light: Limit to most likely probes (intensity 2)
  --version-all: Try every single probe (intensity 9)
  --version-trace: Show detailed version scan activity (for debugging)
SCRIPT SCAN:
  -sC: equivalent to --script=default
  --script=<Lua scripts>: <Lua scripts> is a comma separated list of
            directories, script-files or script-categories
  --script-args=<n1=v1,[n2=v2,...]>: provide arguments to scripts
  --script-args-file=filename: provide NSE script args in a file
  --script-trace: Show all data sent and received
  --script-updatedb: Update the script database.
  --script-help=<Lua scripts>: Show help about scripts.
            <Lua scripts> is a comma separted list of script-files or
            script-categories.
```

OS DETECTION:
  -O: Enable OS detection
  --osscan-limit: Limit OS detection to promising targets
  --osscan-guess: Guess OS more aggressively
TIMING AND PERFORMANCE:
  Options which take <time> are in seconds, or append 'ms' (milliseconds),
  's' (seconds), 'm' (minutes), or 'h' (hours) to the value (e.g. 30m).
  -T<0-5>: Set timing template (higher is faster)
  --min-hostgroup/max-hostgroup <size>: Parallel host scan group sizes
  --min-parallelism/max-parallelism <numprobes>: Probe parallelization
  --min-rtt-timeout/max-rtt-timeout/initial-rtt-timeout <time>: Specifies
      probe round trip time.
  --max-retries <tries>: Caps number of port scan probe retransmissions.
  --host-timeout <time>: Give up on target after this long
  --scan-delay/--max-scan-delay <time>: Adjust delay between probes
  --min-rate <number>: Send packets no slower than <number> per second
  --max-rate <number>: Send packets no faster than <number> per second
FIREWALL/IDS EVASION AND SPOOFING:
  -f; --mtu <val>: fragment packets (optionally w/given MTU)
  -D <decoy1,decoy2[,ME],...>: Cloak a scan with decoys
  -S <IP_Address>: Spoof source address
  -e <iface>: Use specified interface
  -g/--source-port <portnum>: Use given port number
  --data-length <num>: Append random data to sent packets
  --ip-options <options>: Send packets with specified ip options
  --ttl <val>: Set IP time-to-live field
  --spoof-mac <mac address/prefix/vendor name>: Spoof your MAC address
  --badsum: Send packets with a bogus TCP/UDP/SCTP checksum
OUTPUT:
  -oN/-oX/-oS/-oG <file>: Output scan in normal, XML, s|<rIpt kIddi3,
      and Grepable format, respectively, to the given filename.
  -oA <basename>: Output in the three major formats at once
  -v: Increase verbosity level (use -vv or more for greater effect)
  -d: Increase debugging level (use -dd or more for greater effect)
  --reason: Display the reason a port is in a particular state
  --open: Only show open (or possibly open) ports
  --packet-trace: Show all packets sent and received
  --iflist: Print host interfaces and routes (for debugging)
  --log-errors: Log errors/warnings to the normal-format output file
  --append-output: Append to rather than clobber specified output files
  --resume <filename>: Resume an aborted scan
  --stylesheet <path/URL>: XSL stylesheet to transform XML output to HTML
  --webxml: Reference stylesheet from Nmap.Org for more portable XML
  --no-stylesheet: Prevent associating of XSL stylesheet w/XML output

```
MISC:
  -6: Enable IPv6 scanning
  -A: Enable OS detection, version detection, script scanning, and traceroute
  --datadir <dirname>: Specify custom Nmap data file location
  --send-eth/--send-ip: Send using raw ethernet frames or IP packets
  --privileged: Assume that the user is fully privileged
  --unprivileged: Assume the user lacks raw socket privileges
  -V: Print version number
  -h: Print this help summary page.
EXAMPLES:
  nmap -v -A scanme.nmap.org
  nmap -v -sn 192.168.0.0/16 10.0.0.0/8
  nmap -v -iR 10000 -Pn -p 80
SEE THE MAN PAGE (http://nmap.org/book/man.html) FOR MORE OPTIONS AND
EXAMPLES
```

You can get more about Network Mapper in the internet. Please follow these links.

http://nmap.org/
http://nmap.org/book/man.html
https://nmap.org/book/inst-other-platforms.html
https://nmap.org/book/inst-windows.html
https://nmap.org/book/vscan.html

If in your 'Linux' version of default operating system you don't get this listing you can install 'Nmap' by issuing a simple command.

```
sudo apt-get install nmap
```

In your virtual machine if you run kali Linux, you'll find that 'Nmap' has already been installed.

Now after this installtion part is over we can very quickly have a short python script to see how our 'Nmap' module is working.

You've already learned how to use 'nano' text editor on your terminal. So open it up with this command:

```
sudo nano test.py
```

It will first ask for your root password and then open up the nano text editor on your terminal. Write a short script like this:

```
#!/usr/bin/python
import nmap
nm = nmap.PortScannerAsync()
def callback_result(host, scan_result):
    print ('------------------')
    print (host, scan_result)
```

```
nm.scan('127.0.0.1', arguments="-O -v", callback=callback_result)
while nm.still_scanning():
    print("Waiting >>>")
    nm.wait(2)
nm1 = nmap.PortScanner()
a = nm1.nmap_version()
print (a)
```

If you run your 'test.py' script, you'd get this output:

```
Waiting >>>
------------------
('127.0.0.1', None)
(6, 40)
```

It's your localhost address. But we are interested about the remote target.

Run up the kali Linux in your Virual Box and open the 'Tor' browser. Search 'what is my ip address'. It will give you an anonymous IP address all the time. Each time you search that IP address changes.

In your case it may come out as:

```
x.x.xx.xxx
ISP: Some Internet LTD
```

It's usually too far from your original location! Anyway, you can test the IP and see the result. But it's a good practice to test the IP of http://nmap.org

CHAPTER 24

Building an Nmap Network Scanner

Now we're ready to do more network testing using python scripts. And this time we'll try to build up a more robust scanner and we'll also try to detect the open ports and see if there are any vulnerabilities.

Let us write the python script first. And after that we'll see the output. Let us change the 'test.py' script to this:

```python
#!/usr/bin/python
import nmap
nm = nmap.PortScanner()
print (nm.nmap_version())
nm.scan('x.x.xx.xxx', '1-1024', '-v')
print(nm.scaninfo())
print(nm.csv())
```

Here '-v' stands for version and the '1-1024' stands for the range of the port numbers. It's a very small script but see the power of it in the output.

```
hagudu@hagudu-H81M-S1:~$ ./test.py
(6, 40)
{'tcp': {'services': '1-1024', 'method': 'connect'}}
host;hostname;hostname_type;protocol;port;name;state;product;extrainfo;reas
on;version;conf;cpe
x.x.xx.xxx;host3.x0x;PTR;tcp;22;ssh;open;;;syn-ack;;3;
x.x.xx.xxx;host3.x0x;PTR;tcp;25;smtp;open;;;syn-ack;;3;
x.x.xx.xxx;host3.x0x;PTR;tcp;53;domain;open;;;syn-ack;;3;
x.x.xx.xxx;host3.x0x;PTR;tcp;80;http;open;;;syn-ack;;3;
x.x.xx.xxx;host3.x0x;PTR;tcp;137;netbios-ns;filtered;;;no-response;;3;
x.x.xx.xxx;host3.x0x;PTR;tcp;138;netbios-dgm;filtered;;;no-response;;3;
x.x.xx.xxx;host3.x0x;PTR;tcp;139;netbios-ssn;filtered;;;no-response;;3;
x.x.xx.xxx;host3.x0x;PTR;tcp;445;microsoft-ds;filtered;;;no-response;;3;
```

It shows that all together four ports are open. They are: 22, 25, 53 and 80. And the others are filtered.

Before going to test another port and this time we can show the IP as it's of http://nmap.org, let us have a very quick facts about the port terminology. You can also find the legal side of scanning explained here: https://nmap.org/book/legal-issues.html.

Port is an addressable network location. It's ideally implemented inside the operating system and this OS helps us to discriminate web traffic. This traffic is destined for different applications or services, like some for 'mail', some for 'HTTP' and so and so.

Next we're interested about the Port scanning. In one word, it's a type of process and this process usually tries to connect to a number of sequential ports, as you have just seen in the above output. We want to know which ports are open and what services and operating system are behind them.

Let us scan another IP address (http://nmap.org) and in doing that we have changed the python script a little bit.

```
#!/usr/bin/python
import nmap
nm = nmap.PortScanner()
print (nm.nmap_version())
nm.scan('192.168.146.1', '1-1024', '-v')
print(nm.scaninfo())
print(nm.csv())
```

The output is like this:

```
(6, 40)
{'tcp': {'services': '1-1024', 'method': 'connect'}}
host;hostname;hostname_type;protocol;port;name;state;product;extrainfo;reas
on;version;conf;cpe
192.168.146.1;;;tcp;25;smtp;open;;;syn-ack;;3;
192.168.146.1;;;tcp;53;domain;open;;;syn-ack;;3;
192.168.146.1;;;tcp;80;http;open;;;syn-ack;;3;
```

The open ports are 25, 53 and 80. There are no filtered ports showing on this machine.

Let us get all hosts from that IP with a little change in our previous script. This time we reduce the range so that our program won't run for long.

```
#!/usr/bin/python
import nmap
nm = nmap.PortScanner()
print (nm.nmap_version())
nm.scan('192.168.146.1', '22-455', '-v --version-all')
print(nm.all_hosts())
```

We have changed the number of ports in line number five. We also removed last two lines and want to see if we can get more data from that machine.

The output shows that there is only one host.

```
(6, 40)
{'tcp': {'services': '22-455', 'method': 'connect'}}
['192.168.146.1']
```

Let us change and go back to the previous IP and see the output.

```
#!/usr/bin/python
import nmap
nm = nmap.PortScanner()
print (nm.nmap_version())
nm.scan('x.x.xx.xxx', '22-455', '-v --version-all')
print(nm.all_hosts())
```

Nothing changes. The output tells us about the only one host.
There are more to come.
As we want more information we should ideally change our 'test.py' code.

```
#!/usr/bin/python
import nmap
nm = nmap.PortScanner()
print (nm.nmap_version())
nm.scan('192.168.146.1', '22-1024', '-v --version-all')
print (nm.scanstats())
print (nm['192.168.146.1'].state())
print (nm['192.168.146.1'].all_protocols())
print (nm['192.168.146.1']['tcp'].keys())
```

This time the output is more verbose.

```
(6, 40)
{'uphosts': '1', 'timestr': 'Mon Oct  3 09:53:35 2016', 'downhosts': '0',
'totalhosts': '1', 'elapsed': '5.73'}
up
['tcp']
[80, 25, 53]
```

You see that one host is up.
There is no downhosts and the number of total host is 1 as expected. We also see the exact time when the scan is being excuted and the time elapsed.
Let us dig a bit further.
We have used the port range '1-1024'. Normally ports below 1024 are associated with Linux and Unix like services. This operating systems are considered to be vital for essential network functions. For that reason you must have root privileges to assign services to these type of OS.
If you want to go beyond 1024, there are either 'registered' or 'private' ports. Ports between 49152 and 65535 are supposed to be for private use.

Let us consider the first output and try to understand what port is used for what purposes.

```
x.x.xx.xxx;host3.x0x;PTR;tcp;22;ssh;open;;;syn-ack;;3;
x.x.xx.xxx;host3.x0x;PTR;tcp;25;smtp;open;;;syn-ack;;3;
x.x.xx.xxx;host3.x0x;PTR;tcp;53;domain;open;;;syn-ack;;3;
x.x.xx.xxx;host3.x0x;PTR;tcp;80;http;open;;;syn-ack;;3;
x.x.xx.xxx;host3.x0x;PTR;tcp;137;netbios-ns;filtered;;;no-response;;3;
x.x.xx.xxx;host3.x0x;PTR;tcp;138;netbios-dgm;filtered;;;no-response;;3;
x.x.xx.xxx;host3.x0x;PTR;tcp;139;netbios-ssn;filtered;;;no-response;;3;
x.x.xx.xxx;host3.x0x;PTR;tcp;445;microsoft-ds;filtered;;;no-response;;3;
```

Port 22 is used for 'SSH'. It stands for 'Secure Socket Shell'. It's a network protocol with which administrators access a remote computer in a secure way.

Port 25 is for SMTP or mail.

Port 53 stands for DNS Services.

Port 80 is for web traffic.

Port 137, 138 and 139 are grabbed by Microsoft for transporting their NetBIOS protocol over IP based LAN and WAN networks.

Lastly the port 445 is used for Microsoft Directory Services. For further reading about this port you may find this link interesting: https://www.grc.com/port_445.htm.

PART III

CHAPTER 25

■ ■ ■

Protect Anonymity on the Internet

This is very important for ethical hackers. You need to stay anonymous and hide your IP address while you are in the world of ethical hacking. There are several ways to do that. We will discuss in this chapter how we can do that.

There are proxies. It means you are routing through different routers but it could be very slow and not at your hand. Another down side of using proxies is you don't know anything about the other side. You are in the dark about the servers through which your packets are moving. So that could very risky. You may ask why that is dangerous. I would do some kind of "mapping the network" sort of job. It is harmless. Maybe so. But it is not only restricted to that part. Using proxy, you may want to log into some server. Once you have typed in your password, it could be hijacked.

How can you solve this problem?

There is a term: "VPN." You've probably heard of "virtual private network." What is that? It is basically a kind of service that you are using for encrypting your traffic. And it is very fast. In the future, when you work as a professional, you have to hire a VPN service. It is not very costly. For the time being we could do it for free, just for educational purposes.

But once you encrypt your traffic through VPN, it is recognizable. What happens if an agency asks the service providers for your data? Normally, to avoid that you need to be choosy. You need to hire a service from a certain part of the world where privacy is strictly maintained.

But after saying that and hoping for the best, I'd definitely not recommend you to do your white hat ethical hacking using proxies or VPNs. Basically, you may want to do that for bypassing the firewall setting or that sort of thing. Besides, some VPN services don't allow IP addresses to use their services beyond a range. Suppose your IP address belongs outside of that range. But people often use proxies or VPNs—not always for doing something malicious like taking down a server or stealing data. People might want to hide their location just when they are traveling, or that kind of thing. Apparently this type of activity stays within the law.

There is another problem that might crop up while you access a certain type of server that usually allows IP addresses from a certain region. In that case, if you use an IP address from China or Russia, the network administrator would certainly go after you. So it is a consistent problem that keeps coming and tormenting you from time to time and in the coming chapters we would like address those problems.

© Sanjib Sinha 2017

S. Sinha, *Beginning Ethical Hacking with Python*, DOI 10.1007/978-1-4842-2541-7_25

CHAPTER 26

■ ■ ■

Dark Web and Tor

In the mean time we will have a very quick look at the dark web or hidden web. I don't know whether or not you have heard about it before.

The rumor is the "dark web" or "deep web" consists of a major portion of the Internet. It is something like "dark matter" that consists of 97 or 98 percent of the mass of the universe. It is still unknown what it is actually, except for a few things.

People say the dark web is full of information that we usually don't get normally. And you can't access the dark web through your normal browser. You need a special kind of browser to enter into that maze of mysteries.

I should warn you before you try Tor and enter the dark web. There are lots of illegal activities, generally going on outside our normal perception. It could be like human trafficking. It could be like illegal arms dealing. It could be like hiring killers and whatnot. But in this book we are not interested in them. Our main concern is knowledge. We reach there so that we can have an idea what is going actually going on in the dark web.

As an ethical hacker, you need to know everything for one and only one purpose. You need to fight against a malicious attack. You are learning to defend yourself, not attacking somebody. But to defend yourself, you need to know all the tactics that your enemy often uses. Maybe police will seek your help to track down a child abuser. Without knowing the proper character of the dark web, you can't do that. If you don't know how to hide your IP address how could you locate a criminal who is hiding his real location?

Besides, you need to know another important thing. The dark web is not always bad in that sense. You may find many reputed white hat or gray hat hackers in certain forums that are kept completely hidden from the watchful eyes of government agencies. You may find real helpful people over there who may help you solve your problem instantly. Like Wikipedia, there are hidden wiki that we are soon going to see, where you can find a lot of interesting things to learn.

© Sanjib Sinha 2017
S. Sinha, *Beginning Ethical Hacking with Python*, DOI 10.1007/978-1-4842-2541-7_26

Hidden Wikipedia

To read the hidden wiki we need to install the Tor browser. Kali Linux does not come with it by default so you need to install it.

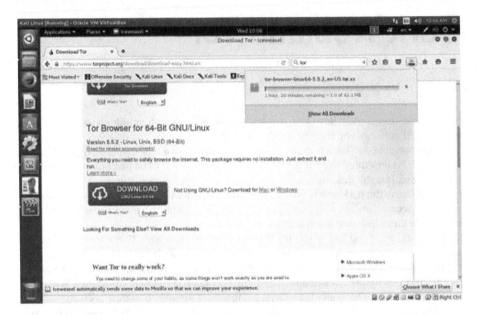

Figure 26-1. *Download section of torproject.org web site*

To do that, first you need to log in as the new user: xman. Then open up the normal browser and search for the Tor browser. Just go to the official site and download the latest version for Kali Linux. Be careful about checking that it is `https://torproject.org`, not anything else. It may come with "http://" without the "s". Simply avoid that.

There are two versions: one is 32 bits and the other is 64 bits. According to your system architecture, you need to download the exact version. Before downloading, it is good practice to learn about Tor from its documentation. There are terms and conditions that you must fulfill. And the main term is you must stay within the law. You can't use Tor for any illegal process. Tor also hides your IP address. But that is a different issue.

Once download is complete, you can access the necessary file in your "Download" folder. Just run it.

Figure 26-2. *Tor browser is connecting.*

Once it is connected, it will open up its default first page, which you would find quite different from the normal browser. First of all, you can type "what is my IP" and check what that shows.

It will definitely be something other than the region where you are. But we need original hidden wiki web pages that will take us to the dark web.

Remember, there are several web sites that claim to be original hidden wiki. So you need to be judicious about choosing. Usually they come with ".onion" domains and the URL is continually changing. So you can type in something like "hidden wiki url" and see what you get.

Figure 26-3. *The original hidden Wiki page*

The main problem is: you can't differentiate the original hidden wiki from the other fake versions. The above image shows how it may look. The extension is always ".onion".

The hidden wiki mainly consists of large amount of various links. Many of them are simply illegal and cheap. It seems like a big market where lots of smuggled goods are sold. Never try to buy anything from here. Though it is tempting to buy something very costly at one third of its original price, it is not certain that it will reach you. Moreover, there is every possibility that your debit or credit number is cracked.

But in this so-called interesting market, there are lots of really useful things that may come to your help. One of them is the forum or chat section where reputed hackers often discuss many interesting things that you don't see usually in any open forum.

At the same time, you need to be careful about using any code coming from these forums or chats just because of the anonymity. It is not advisable to use that code in your original machine.

That could be dangerous!

Let us open up a forum site and see just how it looks. They usually come up with a black background, as if they represent the dark web properly.

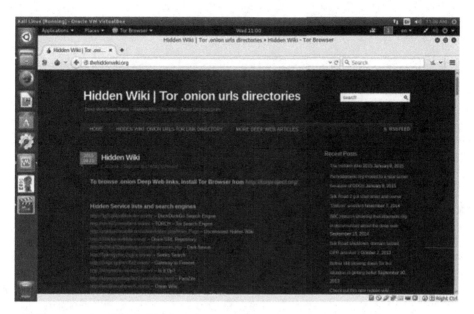

Figure 26-4. *One of the hidden Wiki pages—that could be vague*

One thing you better keep in mind: Tor browser is fine as long as you want to learn something new. It is not meant for doing some dubious things. There are lots of cheap attractions that would definitely try to grab your attention or even force you to go towards them. Be careful about choosing the sites you are visiting. As long as it is a hacker's forum, it is perfectly okay. But once you go beyond the limit without staying within the law, it could be dangerous.

Now we'll move on to things that are more directly connected to real world ethical hacking. But before that, we need to see how proxy chains and VPNs work.

Your little knowledge of Linux commands will come in handy. From now on, everything we do will be on the Kali Linux terminal. So boot up your Kali virtual machine and open up your terminal. First we will learn about proxy chains and, with the help of this tool, how we can hide our IP address and gain access to a remote server.

CHAPTER 27

Proxy Chains

The name suggests its true meaning. To keep anonymity we need several proxies. Behind these proxies we can hide our true identity. It is not successful all the time. But Kali Linux gives you a special opportunity to change the configuration at the root so that you can hide your true identity while browsing the web using Tor. Actually, in this case you need to configure your "prxychain.conf" file. You have already installed Tor.

We need to open up the configuration file using "nano" text editor.

Open up your Kali Linux terminal as a root user and write down this command.

root@kali:~# nano /etc/proxychains.conf

It will open up the "proxychains.conf" file. There are three types of proxies that you can use. But you can't use all the proxies at the same time. Let us first see how this file looks. It is 68 lines long. But it is not very complicated if you understand the lines. The documentations are clear and to the point. Here are the first few important lines.

```
# The option below identifies how the ProxyList is treated.
# only one option should be uncommented at time,
# otherwise the last appearing option will be accepted
#
dynamic_chain
#
# Dynamic - Each connection will be done via chained proxies
# all proxies chained in the order as they appear in the list
# at least one proxy must be online to play in chain
# (dead proxies are skipped)
# otherwise EINTR is returned to the app
```

What does this mean? It says the proxy list has several options. You must know how you should treat these options. If you read every line, you'd get an idea how it works. There are three types of proxies. You need to uncomment any one of them.

© Sanjib Sinha 2017
S. Sinha, *Beginning Ethical Hacking with Python*, DOI 10.1007/978-1-4842-2541-7_27

The first proxy is "dynamic-chain". You see the line above and the red color shows that I have uncommented it. There are two more proxies: "strict_chain" and "random_chain". They are commented out. They have their own descriptions. Let us read them both.

```
#strict_chain
#
# Strict - Each connection will be done via chained proxies
# all proxies chained in the order as they appear in the list
# all proxies must be online to play in chain
# otherwise EINTR is returned to the app
#
#random_chain
#
# Random - Each connection will be done via random proxy
# (or proxy chain, see  chain_len) from the list.
# this option is good to test your IDS :)
```

It is described clearly in the documentation that comes up along with it. So I don't elaborate it again. The advantage of choosing "dynamic_chain" over others is clearly stated. If your connection does not get one "working proxy" then it automatically jumps to the other. The other two don't give you that opportunity to route your traffic.

Let me explain it more. Suppose you have two proxies in place: A and B. What happens in the case of "strict_chain" is that when you browse web pages, your connection is routed through A and B strictly. It means A and B should be in order and live. Otherwise your connection simply fails. In the case of "dynamic_chain" this does not happen. If A is down then it jumps to take B. It works that way.

I hope the first step is clear. Let us consider a few other important steps.

In between you get a line like this:

```
# Proxy DNS requests - no leak for DNS data
proxy_dns
```

It is a very important line to be considered seriously. You see I have uncommented the "proxy_dns". You can't allow DNS data to be leaked. In other words, your real IP address should not be leaked by any chance. That is why I have uncommented this line, so that your proxies are in proper place working without any hitch.

At the end of the list you'd find this line:

```
[ProxyList]
# add proxy here ...
# meanwile
# defaults set to "tor"
socks4  127.0.0.1        9050
socks5  127.0.0.1        9050

socks5 185.43.7.146      1080
socks5 75.98.148.183     45021
```

Please inspect the last two lines in red. I have added them. Let me explain why I added them. But before doing that, I'd like to explain the example lines just given before. They read like this:

```
# ProxyList format
#       type  host  port [user pass]
#       (values separated by 'tab' or 'blank')
#
#
#       Examples:
#
#             socks5  192.168.67.78  1080    lamer   secret
#             http    192.168.89.3   8080    justu   hidden
#             socks4  192.168.1.49   1080
#             http    192.168.39.93  8080
```

It clearly states how your proxy list should be formatted. Consider the first line:

```
#             socks5  192.168.67.78  1080    lamer   secret
```

It means: the first one is the "type" of the proxy. It should be "socks5". The second one is: "host". The third one is "port" and the last two words stand for "username" and "password" in case you pay for it. Another important thing is: you must separate the words either by using "tab" or by pressing "blank".

There are several free proxies you'd find so don't bother about the last two right now. Now we can again go back to the last lines that we have been discussing. In the last lines it has been mentioned that "defaults set to tor".

Before adding the last two lines you need to add this line:

```
socks5  127.0.0.1          9050
```

We should do that because usually your "proxychains.conf" file comes up with only "socks4", so you need to add "socks5", which supports present modern technology. Now you can test your "Tor" status.

Open up your terminal and type: ***service tor status***
It will fail if you don't start it. So type: ***service tor start***
It will start the service.

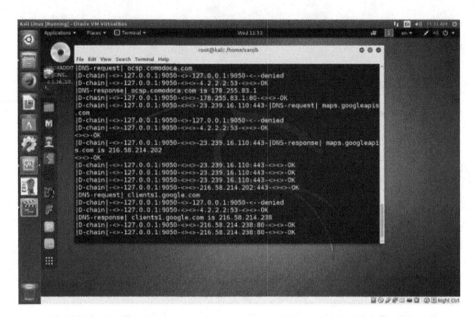

Figure 27-1. *Tor is running through the terminal*

And you can open up your browser through the terminal. Just type: ***proxychains firefox** **www.duckduckgo.com*** http://www.duckduckgo.com/

This search engine does not usually track IP addresses. Your browser will open up and you can check your IP addressIP address. We would also like to see the DNS leak test result. Let us do that by typing "dns leak test" in the search engine. There are several services; you can click any one of them to see what it says.

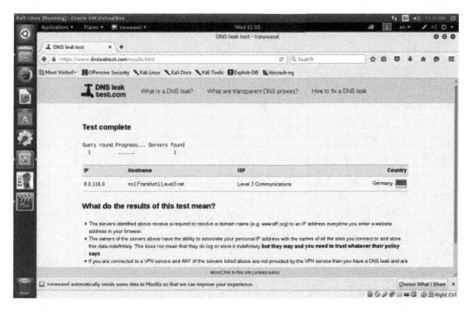

Figure 27-2. DNS leak test

I found the "www.dnsleaktest.com" is working to find out my original IP address and fails to find out. It shows an IP like "8.0.116.0" and it is from Germany. This is wrong, as I am writing this near Calcutta.

You can simultaneously test the same in your normal browser and you'll find your actual IP address.

CHAPTER 28

■ ■ ■

Virtual Private Network or VPN

From the very beginning I try to emphasize one thing. Ethical hacking starts with one single concept: anonymity.

You first must ensure that you're anonymous. You have left no trace behind your back. Your whole journey is hidden and no one can trace your route later.

We have discussed "Tor" browser and "proxy chains". We have seen how we can use them. Another very important concept in this regard is virtual private network or VPN, for short.

It basically deals with the DNS server settings. A DNS server normally checks the traffic filtering. So if you can change your DNS server setting in your root, you can misguide that reading.

How can we do that?

Open your Kali Linux terminal and type:

```
cat /etc/resolv.conf
```

It will show something like this:

```
# Generated by NetworkManager
nameserver 192.168.1.1
```

In your terminal there is every possibility that it'd show something else. This is your home gateway, what kind of router you're using; it is just showing that information. Basically we're going to change this so that when we again test our IP address, the DNS server can't filter the traffic properly.

In my terminal when I type the same command, it reads like this:

```
nameserver 208.67.222.222
nameserver 208.67.220.220
```

If you guessed that I had actually changed this, you are right. I have changed it. Why I have changed this? Let me explain.

S. Sinha, *Beginning Ethical Hacking with Python*, DOI 10.1007/978-1-4842-2541-7_28

You need to understand the concept of "nameserver" first. What does it do? The LAN IP address actually forwards the traffic to DNS servers, which in turn resolve the queries and send the traffic back accordingly.

In doing this it also records the amount of traffic you are having through your home gateway. We don't need that. Why don't we need that? We need to be anonymous. So that is the main reason behind changing this name server.

We can do that through virtual private network or VPN.

Let us open the terminal again and type in this command:

nano /etc/dhcp/dhclient.conf

It will open the configuration file where we will change the name server address. Let us see how it looks.

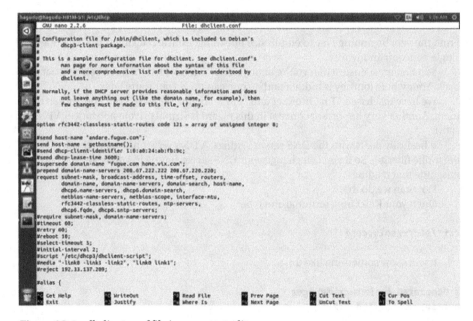

Figure 28-1. *dhclient.conf file in nano text editor*

I've opened it on my Ubuntu terminal. But you need to change it on your Kali Linux virtual machine. You notice that there are lots of things written over there. But we're interested about this line in between:

prepend domain-name-servers 127.0.0.1;

We'll uncomment this line first and then change it. There are lots of OpenDNS IP addresses available on the web. Search with the term "opendns" and it will open up a lot of options from where you can copy the OpenDNS addresses. One of them is "opendns. com". Let us copy two addresses from it and just paste them in place of 127.0.0.1 like this:

```
prepend domain-name-servers 208.67.222.222 208.67.220.220;
```

Now all you need to do is one thing. You've got to restart the network manager. Type this command on your Kali Linux terminal:

service network-manager restart

Now you can check your name server again. It'll show two new addresses.

Another thing is important here. You need to check whether the media connection is enabled or not. Open your Mozilla browser (in Kali Linux it is "Iceweasel"). You find it on top left panel.

Open the browser and type in "about:config". It looks like this:

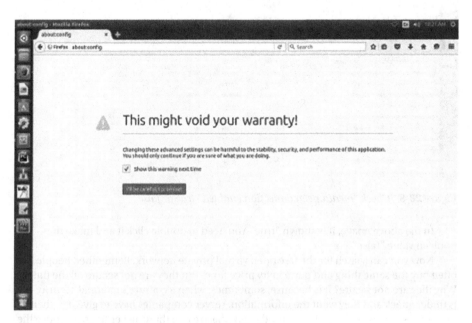

Figure 28-2. about:config image on your Mozilla browser

If you use Chrome or Opera, this will show something else. You need to click and enter into it. Entering into it will assure you a search panel on the top where you will enter the search term: "media.peerconnection.enabled".

Let us see how it looks.

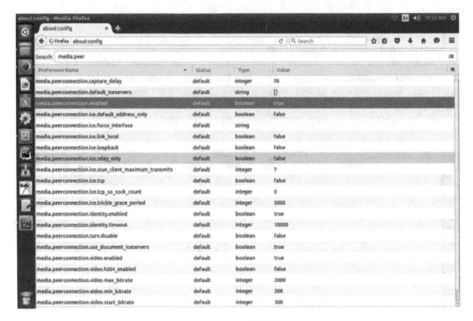

Figure 28-3. *Check "media.peerconnection.enabled" true or false*

In the above image, it is shown "true". You need to double click it and make the Boolean value "false".

Now you can search for the free open virtual private network. Remember, people often buy the same thing and pay a hefty price for it. But they are not secure all the time. Why they are not secure? It is because, sometimes, when a country's national security is under attack and they want the information, server companies have to give it to them under pressure. So all along I have tried to emphasize one thing: never try to go above the law. Ethical hacking is all about something that strictly maintains one and only principle: staying within law.

You learn everything for your self-defense, not for any kind of attack in advance. Anyway, in this chapter our main target is how we can hide the DNS server from our ISP provider.

We have searched about open VPN and found "www.vpnbook.com". We are going to download from this site. On the right-hand panel, you'll find the name of the providers. It varies from time to time. From which country you'll download really doesn't matter as long as it works.

While downloading you'll notice that a combination of username and password is given. Copy them and save them somewhere as you'll need them when you run virtual private network in your machine.

In the download section of your Kali Linux you have a zipped version of VPN. Unzip it first and then run it. How you can do that? Let me open my Kali Linux "Download" section and see what I see.

```
sanjib@kali:~$ cd Downloads/
sanjib@kali:~/Downloads$ ls
vpnbook-euro1-tcp443.ovpn
vpnbook-euro1-tcp80.ovpn
vpnbook-euro1-udp25000.ovpn
vpnbook-euro1-udp53.ovpn
```

To get the same output, you have to unzip your VPN zipped version. Now issue this command:

```
openvpn vpnbook-euro1-tcp443.ovpn
```

If the machine said, "openvpn command not found", you would have to install it. Installing anything through the terminal is quite easy in Linux. Search over the web; there are tons of tutorials that will guide you about that. Usually it is done by the "apt-get" command.

When you try to run "openvpn" it will ask for the username first. Then it'll ask for the password. Once this process is complete, it'll try to build the connection. You need to wait for some time. Unless you get a message, "initialization complete", you can't open your browser. It may take several minutes. Usually it takes two minutes minimum.

If you're not lucky, it may be some time—not always, of course. This message won't crop up. In that case, it says, "connection failed".

Once you get the message, "initialization complete", you can open the browser and search through "www.duckduckgo.com". This search engine usually doesn't track the user's record.

Your first job will be checking the DNS leak. Go for it and you'll definitely find a changed IP address.

It means you have successfully connected through the virtual private network and your original ISP DNS server is completely hidden.

CHAPTER 29

■ ■ ■

MAC Address

We have learned many tricks so far—all about anonymity. But we'll always try to go to a higher level. Changing the MAC address falls into that category.

In a simple way, it is your hardware address. Basically, it's not the hardware address of your machine, but it's the hardware address of your network card through which you're connected to the outer world.

Let us start our Kali Linux virtual machine and open up the terminal. Issue the command: **ipconfig**.

It'll produce something like this:

```
root@kali:~# ifconfig
eth0: flags=4163<UP,BROADCAST,RUNNING,MULTICAST>  mtu 1500      inet
10.0.2.15  netmask 255.255.255.0  broadcast 10.0.2.255  inet6
e80::a00:27ff:fef4:16ec  prefixlen 64  scopeid 0x20<link>
ether 08:00:27:f4:16:ec  txqueuelen 1000  (Ethernet)     RX packets 19  bytes
1820 (1.7 KiB) RX errors 0  dropped 0  overruns 0  frame 0              TX
packets 31  bytes 2427 (2.3 KiB)    TX errors 0  dropped 0 overruns 0
carrier 0  collisions 0

lo:
flags=73<UP,LOOPBACK,RUNNING>  mtu 65536         inet 127.0.0.1  netmask
255.0.0.0   inet6 ::1 prefixlen 128  scopeid 0x10<host>  loop  txqueuelen 0
(Local Loopback)  RX packets 36  bytes 2160 (2.1 KiB)   RX errors 0  dropped
0  overruns 0  frame 0          TX packets 36  bytes 2160 (2.1 KiB)  TX errors
0  dropped 0 overruns 0  carrier 0  collisions 0
```

In your case, the output could be different. We're concerned about the hardware address of our network and we want to change it.

In between, you've seen the red colored line that reads: **ether 08:00:27:f4:16:ec**

This is Kali Linux virtual machine's MAC address or local network card address. Now in some cases it might be like this: **HWaddr 08:00:27:f4:16:ec**

In some cases it is different. They are network cards. They could be Ethernet cards, wireless cards, wireless adapters, etcetera.

But this address is extremely important, as it is used to identify you in the vast web world. The first three digits are the symbols that represent the manufacturer.

© Sanjib Sinha 2017
S. Sinha, *Beginning Ethical Hacking with Python*, DOI 10.1007/978-1-4842-2541-7_29

We can check it out here also by issuing this command:

```
root@kali:~# macchanger -s eth0
Current MAC:   08:00:27:f4:16:ec (CADMUS COMPUTER SYSTEMS)
Permanent MAC: 08:00:27:f4:16:ec (CADMUS COMPUTER SYSTEMS)
```

As you see, it shows two MAC address—one is current and the other is permanent. You may ask why I'm checking this here. I have checked it once by issuing command "ifconfig". Isn't that enough?

It's because the command "ifconfig" will only show the current MAC address. It won't show the permanent MAC address. It means when you have changed the MAC address and issued the "ifconfig" command, it only show the changed one, not the permanent one.

Now we'd like to change our MAC address. Let us issue this command:

```
root@kali:~# macchanger -h
```

And it will produce an output like this:

```
GNU MAC Changer
Usage: macchanger [options] device

  -h, --help                Print this help
  -V, --version             Print version and exit
  -s, --show                Print the MAC address and exit
  -e, --ending              Don't change the vendor bytes
  -a, --another   Set random vendor MAC of the same kind
  -A                        Set random vendor MAC of any kind
  -p, --permanent           Reset to original, permanent hardware MAC
  -r, --random              Set fully random MAC
  -l, --list[=keyword]      Print known vendors
  -b, --bia                 Pretend to be a burned-in-address
  -m, --mac=XX:XX:XX:XX:XX:XX
      --mac XX:XX:XX:XX:XX:XX  Set the MAC XX:XX:XX:XX:XX:XX
```

Report bugs to https://github.com/alobbs/macchanger/issues

The three red-colored lines are important. It is explicitly defined what they mean. The green colored line is also important.

The first two lines— -a, --another Set random vendor MAC of the same kind

-A Set random vendor MAC of any kind

—mean you can change the MAC address but you can't change the vendor. In this case, there is every possibility of losing your anonymity. The first three sets belong to the net card manufacturer and, since that has not been changed, you can be identified.

The third red-colored line is quite obvious and self-explanatory in its meaning. It says: you can change back to the original MAC address.

So far, the best option available for us is the green colored line— -r, --random   Set fully random MAC—where it is clearly said that you can set fully random MAC. That is, the six sets are completely random—which we prefer.

The most important of them is the last blue-colored line. Why is it important? It is because you can change the MAC address completely.

We can have a list of all vendors with a simple command: l. If you issue that command it will give a very long list. Let us pick up a few of them.

```
root@kali:~# macchanger -l

Misc MACs:

Num     MAC         Vendor

---     ---         ------

0000 - 00:00:00 - XEROX CORPORATION

0001 - 00:00:01 - XEROX CORPORATION

0002 - 00:00:02 - XEROX CORPORATION

0003 - 00:00:03 - XEROX CORPORATION

0004 - 00:00:04 - XEROX CORPORATION

0005 - 00:00:05 - XEROX CORPORATION

0006 - 00:00:06 - XEROX CORPORATION

0007 - 00:00:07 - XEROX CORPORATION

0008 - 00:00:08 - XEROX CORPORATION

0009 - 00:00:09 - XEROX CORPORATION

0010 - 00:00:0a - OMRON TATEISI ELECTRONICS CO.

0011 - 00:00:0b - MATRIX CORPORATION

0012 - 00:00:0c - CISCO SYSTEMS, INC.

0013 - 00:00:0d - FIBRONICS LTD.

0014 - 00:00:0e - FUJITSU LIMITED

0015 - 00:00:0f - NEXT, INC.

0016 - 00:00:10 - SYTEK INC.

0017 - 00:00:11 - NORMEREL SYSTEMES

0018 - 00: 00:12 - INFORMATION TECHNOLOGY LIMITED

0019 - 00:00:13 - CAMEX
```

We have taken first few lines—nineteen at present. But the last one is **19010 - fc:fe:77 - Hitachi Reftechno, Inc.** The red-colored number shows how many there are altogether. The list is not complete. After that, there are wireless MAC addresses. There are altogether around thirty-nine.

You may ask what they are actually. They are nothing but the bits of the company MAC address. Let us consider the last example: **0019 - 00:00:13 – CAMEX.**

The first one is the serial number. The second one is the MAC address. You can change your vendor address and use this one and pretend to be using this company. Ethical hackers sometime use that trick.

Keeping everything in mind, I'd like to say that the last option—the blue-colored one—is the most important.

In colleges, students sometimes use that trick to fool the professor, along with the whole class. Someone takes the professor's MAC address and, pretending to be the professor's PC, he jams the network. Once the network has been jammed, the teacher can't take the class anymore.

Usually there is a network filtering system that finds out the rogue MAC address and blocks that address. But that is also fun. When the network filtering system has blocked the MAC address, it comes out that the professor's PC has been blocked inadvertently.

As an ethical hacker you need to study this part particularly, as the malicious hackers often use another's machine MAC address and pretend to be someone while they do the wrong things.

Epilogue—What Next

Thanks for reading this volume of *Ethical Hacking with Python 3*. I hope that, as a beginner, you have learned the basics of ethical hacking. That includes the terms, legal side, and purpose; networking, the environment, and a detailed introduction on anonymity. Additionally, I hope that you have a working knowledge of Python 3.

The next volumes of books on Ethical Hacking will deal with more advanced concepts like "Nmap," "SQL Injection," "Denial of Service or DOS," "Brute Force Method," "Signal Jamming," "Password Cracking," "Footprinting with Nmap," "Attacking Wireless Networks," "WiFi Hacking, Breaking Encryptions", "SLl Strips" and many more.

Hope to meet you in the next book. Till then, **best of luck**.

© Sanjib Sinha 2017
195
S. Sinha, *Beginning Ethical Hacking with Python*, DOI 10.1007/978-1-4842-2541-7

Index

© Sanjib Sinha 2017
S. Sinha, *Beginning Ethical Hacking with Python*, DOI 10.1007/978-1-4842-2541-7

■ W, X, Y, Z

Get the eBook for only $4.99!

Why limit yourself?

Now you can take the weightless companion with you wherever you go and access your content on your PC, phone, tablet, or reader.

Since you've purchased this print book, we are happy to offer you the eBook for just $4.99.

Convenient and fully searchable, the PDF version enables you to easily find and copy code—or perform examples by quickly toggling between instructions and applications.

To learn more, go to http://www.apress.com/us/shop/companion or contact support@apress.com.

Printed in the United States
By Bookmasters